CHINESE
EMBROIDERY
TRADITIONAL TECHNIQUES

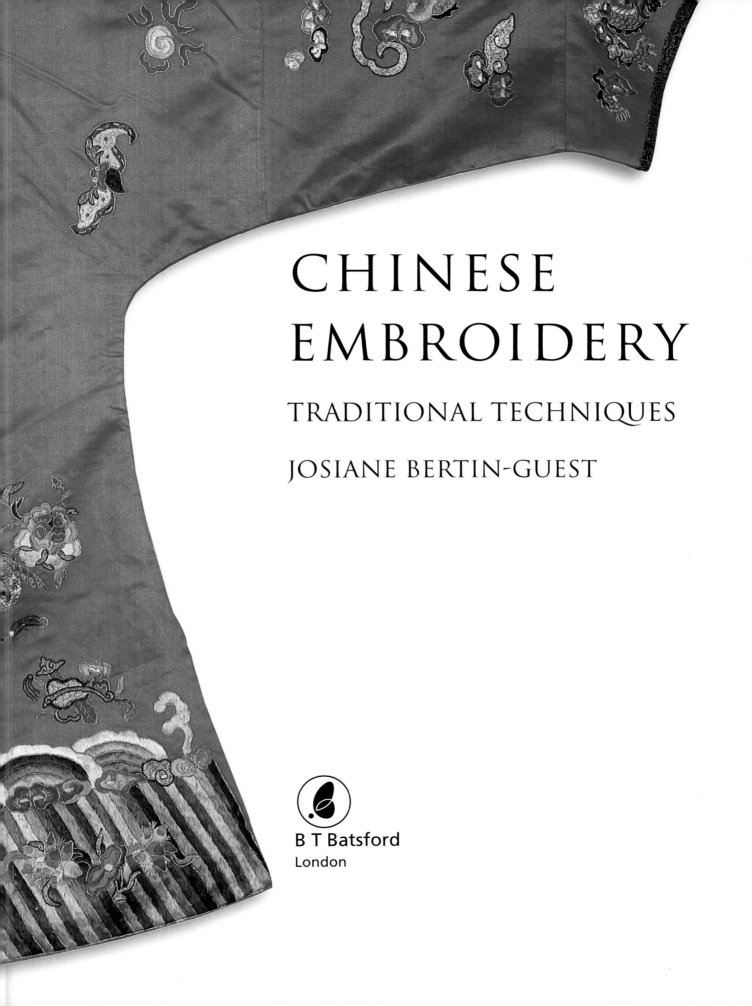

CHINESE
EMBROIDERY

TRADITIONAL TECHNIQUES

JOSIANE BERTIN-GUEST

B T Batsford
London

To Steven, Kevin and Kenny

First published 2003

© Josiane Bertin-Guest 2003

The right of Josiane Bertin-Guest to be identified
as Author of this work has been asserted to her in accordance
with the Copyright, Designs and Patents Act 1988.

ISBN 0 7134 8779 8

A CIP catalogue record for this book is
available from the British Library.

Photography by Michael Wicks except where stated.

Printed in Italy by Canale

for the publishers
B T Batsford
64 Brewery Road
London
N7 9NT
www.batsford.com

A member of Chrysalis Books plc

Contents

Half-title page *Embroidered panel, early 20th century, featuring a pair of lions playing with a ball, surrounded by chrysanthemum, lotus, peony and finger lemon flowers.* Title page *Woman's dragon jacket of red satin, dating from c. 1872.* Right and opposite page *Exquisite embroidery from a woman's robe, early 19th century, depicting a butterfly in block shading stitch.*

Preface

This book came about as a result of my search for step-by-step instructions on traditional Chinese embroidery and for specific information relating to this subject. Unable to find a comprehensive volume on the subject, I began to assemble the necessary information. Unfortunately, although my research on Chinese embroidery started some 25 years ago, for one reason or another, I lacked the time to edit the general notes accumulated over the years, and they were relegated to a back drawer. A few years ago, however, during a visit to China, I had the opportunity to embroider with friends who had trained at the Institute of Embroidery in Suzhou. Inspired again, I returned to London intent on resurrecting, updating and editing my research notes.

By no means should this volume be regarded as a definitive work on the subject of traditional Chinese embroidery; this would be an unmanageably vast subject, due to the abundance of styles and techniques that stem from all the different regions of China. This research concentrates on one style of embroidery – the Imperial style – which is found mainly on textiles of the Qing Dynasty (1644–1911). Examples of this style may still be purchased today; certain antique pieces from my own collection and those of other private collectors have been photographed, and their reproduction explained in a clear step-by-step approach, accompanied by line drawings of the originals. This book is therefore intended to provide an informative, aesthetic and practical approach to some of the popular techniques found in traditional Chinese embroidery. The stitches used have been translated, where possible, to their appropriate equivalents in the western dictionary of embroidery stitches, and some of their Chinese language equivalents have been noted.

For the practicalities of this book, the use of metal threads (goldwork) and double-sided embroidery have only been touched upon lightly. These are subject matters entirely in their own right and will be addressed more fully in the future.

It is not intended that the visual instructions laid out in this volume should be adhered to rigidly. Individual embroiderers develop their own approach, style and method of work, as there are numerous ways in which any motif or design can be interpreted and executed. The brief introduction to the historical development of Chinese embroidery, together with recurrent motifs and symbols used in the general designs, will hopefully serve only as guidelines, fuelling the imagination and inviting the reader to take an individual journey, exploring the techniques found in Chinese embroidery.

Opposite page *Vase with flower from a woman's waistcoat, 19th century. The design has been embroidered, then glued to several layers of paper, cut up and appliquéd onto the waistcoat.*

Acknowledgments

This book would not have been published but for the group of people involved with it at various stages of my research.

First of all, I am indebted to the older generation of my family, mainly my grandmother Irene Eupercile Bertin-Legris, who taught me the rudiments of sewing, embroidery and appreciation of various creative crafts, my mother Gladys Bertin-Lavictoire and my aunts Raymonde Bertin-Lecerf and Arlette Bertin-Fournier, who kept me busy with every type of embroidery project (some of them undertaken grudgingly) all through my childhood and teenage years.

My thanks also to the close circle of friends who have encouraged me to put pen to paper and given me unconditional support throughout the editing of the script: my childhood friend Danielle Arouff-Blake, who travelled regularly back and forth from Kansas City to offer support; for their embroidery expertise, advice and down-to-earth practical sense, Pattie Dougill-Goudie, Elizabeth Dudley and Cecilia Hankin; my teacher Dorothy Tucker, for her belief in my creative ability and her staunch support in all aspects of creative work over 20 years. Great thanks are due to my Chinese friends and embroidery teachers: namely, Zhang Gwa, Ling Ling and Mrs Zhang, who guided me through the maze of design and embroidery stitches, and Mr Wu, the artist, for his picture of the cranes that he so kindly gave me. I would also like to thank the team at Batsford, including Tina Persaud, Nicola Birtwisle and Dave Crook. Finally, this book owes much to my husband, Steven and my twin sons Kevin and Kenny, and Kevin's partner Alison, whose loyalty and support during the hectic moments were much appreciated.

Above *Pair of mandarin ducks, Jiangsu province, 21st century. Modern embroidery in rich, bright colours from a satin silk bedcover, made for the tourist and export market. The techniques used include stem stitch, satin stitch, block shading, encroaching and overlaid stitches.*
Right *Detail of subtle satin stitch shading on a duck's wing.*
Opposite page *Chinese silk threads and de Havilland spaced dyed threads.*

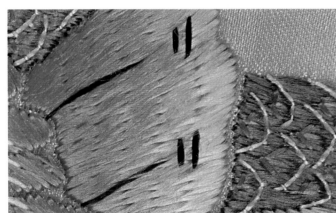

Introduction

Since my early childhood, the beauty of Chinese embroidery as well as other forms of Chinese art has fascinated me. Though many books have been written on the subject of Chinese art and textiles, there are a limited few detailing the methods of work and techniques of Chinese embroidery. My research highlighted a need for a specific book that would bring together most of the traditional techniques found on antique examples of Chinese textiles, and the development and progression of traditional embroidery within China today.

It would be impractical to attempt to cover in one book the huge variety of styles and techniques that may be found in traditional Chinese embroidery, stemming from all the different areas of China. The embroidery covered in this book therefore relates mainly to the style prevalent in the Qing Dynasty period, while combining elements that are characteristic of the styles of different regions. For the purpose of this book, the term 'Imperial style of embroidery' has been loosely applied. On this basis, the book aims to provide the beginner and the advanced embroiderer with technical step-by–step instructions on how to create and achieve some of the beautiful embroidery techniques found on pieces from that period. There is also a brief summary of the subsequent development of this style of embroidery as it is currently found in China today.

The general information laid out in this book was gathered from various sources, including museums, private collections and several key authors in the field of Chinese art, textiles and embroidery. Invaluable insights have been gleaned from close observation of damaged pieces of antique Chinese embroidery dating from the early 18th to the late 19th centuries. These samples have been of enormous help in identifying the variety of styles, techniques, methods of work and applications, types of fabrics, threads, designs and colours used. The overall research, illustrations and methods of work have been combined with practical experiments and stitching sessions, undertaken both here and in China.

The various designs and diagrams are drawn from my personal collection of antique and modern samples of Chinese textiles, with a few pieces from private collectors.

Left Multicoloured shawl, 20th century. A typical shawl made for export, also referred to as a Spanish shawl. The bright chinoiserie landscape design with pagodas and people has been hand-embroidered with commercially twisted silk. The knotted fringe (which, on this type of shawl, were not always made with silk threads) tends to be very heavy and so the shawl is not very practical to wear. These shawls are sometimes used as decorative table covers or throws.

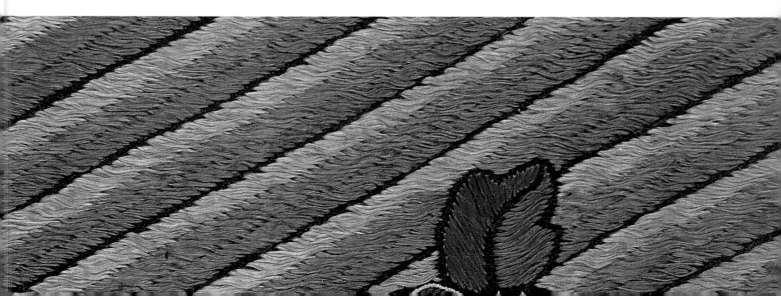

Chapter One
History and development of Chinese embroidery

The development of embroidery as an advanced art form has been attributed to China, where its history spans some 4,000 years. It is difficult to ascertain precisely when embroidery started in China, as our information is dependent on archaeological excavations and ancient writings. To date, researchers have established that Chinese embroidery began at around the time of the Shang Dynasty (*c.* 1600 BC–1027 BC).

The introduction of silk

Silk forms a quintessential part of Chinese embroidery as we know it today, but prior to the discovery of silk in around 700 BC, cloth was made from hemp and other plant fibres. Hemp threads were also used to stitch and decorate the fabric, and further decoration could be added with the use of a variety of drilled shells, beads and mother-of-pearl plaques. The earliest needles were made of bone.

Silk played a vital role in the evolution of embroidery. There are many versions of the story of its discovery and subsequent development across the continents, and the possibility that fact and fiction may have merged over the years could account for these anomalies. In one account, the discovery of silk is attributed to a 14-year-old concubine of the legendary Yellow Emperor, namely the Empress Hsi-Ling Lo-tsu. Apparently, she was taking tea under a mulberry tree when a cocoon accidentally fell into her cup of tea and in retrieving the worm she unwound the secret of silk. The empress has also been regarded as the person who promoted the rearing of silkworms. It has been written that the secret of silk was jealously guarded until it reached the kingdom of Khotan, Tibet, in 140 BC, when silkworm eggs were smuggled in the headdress of a Chinese princess who had married a prince of Khotan.

Above *Hanks and skeins of Chinese silk thread, which can be split into extremely fine filaments for fine embroidery.*

Another tale that has been passed down about the origins of silk is that some time around AD 550, Emperor Justinian of the Byzantine Empire sent two Persian monks to Khotan (now in Xinjiang province, western China) to find out the secret of this mysterious new fibre. The monks returned first with mulberry seeds and later with several silkworms hidden in a bamboo stick, which they smuggled via Korea to Japan. Emperor Justinian, in his turn, tried to guard the secret of silk, but by the 9th century AD, the knowledge of silk and how to produce it had reached Europe. Historians have subsequently named the channel to the West that was used by silk traders as the Silk Road.

Silk fibre is the product of several silkworms of the *Bombycidae* and *Saturniidae* genera. Of all the silkworm species, *Bombyx mori* is particularly favoured because of the strength, fineness and consistency of filament of the silk it produces. The single silk filaments are reeled when cocoons are immersed in boiling water. The length of filament from a single cocoon can measure as much as 450–1,800 metres (1,476–5,905 feet).

Early embroideries

The earliest known description of Chinese embroidery is written in the classical text *Shangshu* (Book of History), compiled during the Western Zhou period (1027–771 BC). This book laid out the regulations that applied some 4,000 years ago to the making and wearing of garments, including the more decorative aspects of design and embroidery.

Another reference to early embroidery can be found in the *Zhou Li* (Rites of Zhou), an Eastern Zhou record dating back to before the Warring States period (475–221 BC). It describes how 'whatever is embroidered needs to be painted, whereafter it may be stitched', thus indicating

even at this early time the close links that were later to develop between embroidery and painting.

From evidence gathered by the research undertaken following the discovery of several pieces of embroidery in the Mawangdui caves in Hunan province, it is thought that workrooms with trained embroiderers were in existence in the second century BC. The embroiderers were trained in their craft from early childhood, and the techniques they used were probably handed down by word of mouth from generation to generation. Embroidery may have been carried out by both men and women, either working individually at home or in a group within a studio environment. Only the best and most fully experienced embroiderers worked on the more complicated designs, and two or more embroiderers would work on a large-scale piece. During this time, women not only raised silkworms at home but also reeled the cocoons, and the silk was then used for the embroidery with which they earned their living.

Some of the oldest surviving pieces of embroidery, which were unearthed in 1958 from tombs in the state of Zhou, are reported to date back to the Warring States Period (475–221 BC) and have been identified as belonging to the Xiang style of embroidery from the Hunan area of China.

Archaeological textiles from funerary tombs in Baoji City, Shaanxi Province have been dated to the early Western Zhou period (1027–771 BC). The fragmented pieces of embroidery that were found in these tombs carried designs of flying dragons, ferocious tigers, dancing phoenix-like birds and other auspicious animals, birds and flowers, as well as stylized geometric vine patterns. The predominant stitches used on these pieces of embroidery were chain stitch, braided chain stitch and also split stitch. Chain stitch was used either to outline a design or, more popularly, the motifs were entirely covered in the stitch to provide a rich visual effect.

Above *A 19th-century example of couched peacock feathers.*

Chinese embroidered silks have also been discovered in the Scythian tombs of the Altai Mountains in Eastern Siberia by the Russian archaeologist Sergei Rudenko. Some of the textiles contain chain stitch embroidery on silk plain weave. The embroidered textiles, with designs of a stylized long-tailed bird among curving branches, exotic flowers and leaves, are described as having been casually pieced together by their barbarian owners to make a saddle cover.

Other embroidered pieces, discovered in 1972 in Mawangdui No.1 Han Tomb near Changsha, Hunan Province, were well preserved, showing bright colours. The embroidery, dating from the second century BC, was worked in wool needlepoint, chain stitch and braided chain stitch. At the time of their discovery, the various types of embroidery were classified according to their decorative style and patterns. The pieces were therefore named according to their visual designs, with names such as 'longevity embroidery', 'cloud-riding embroidery' or 'silkworm-veined embroidery'. Reproductions of some of these embroidered patterns are preserved at the Suzhou Embroidery Research Institute.

Several pieces of embroidered textiles, again from the second century BC, described as sophisticated and flawlessly executed in chain stitches with tendril designs and stylized birds, were also unearthed from the tomb of a female commoner in Mashan, Hubei province in 1982.

Another piece noteworthy of mention is the silk-embroidered image of Buddha discovered in the Mogao Grottoes, Dunhuang, Gansu province. Reported to date back to the Wei Dynasties, between 386 and 556 AD, this embroidery is classified as one of the earliest pieces produced purely for appreciation rather than to embellish practical items.

References to embroidery, and to one of the very few ladies whose work is mentioned in the history of Chinese embroidery, may be found in the *Shih I chi,* written by Wang Jia. This states that a certain Lady Chao was commissioned by the hegemon of the kingdom of Wu to make embroidered representations of mountains and streams, physical terrain and battle formations. Unfortunately, no examples of this type of work are known to have survived.

Sometimes other elements, such as the feathers of peacocks or fighting cocks, were incorporated into an embroidery. The feathers were broken down into strands and were either used on their own or blended with silk and gold threads, then couched down. Above left is an example of peacock feathers that have been couched to decorate the head of a dragon (see page 94).

Symbols and designs

Generally, Chinese embroidered textiles are filled with symbols and meanings expressed through the play on words found in rebus motifs, maxims, design and colour. Chinese mythology, and the religious beliefs of Taoism and Buddhism, were also influential on the designs of animals, birds, butterflies, flowers and figures, which were mixed, stylized and transformed.

Certain plants and flowers used in Chinese designs would have specific birds associated and represented with them.

- Peony with long-tailed birds such as peacock, phoenix, fowl and the pheasant
- Lotus with ducks
- Willow with swallow
- Millet with quails and partridge
- Pine with the stork

Designs, for example those found on sleevebands, could combine the theme of nature with landscapes and figure drawings. The designs might either be embroidered in a one-stitch technique or combine a multitude of stitches and techniques.

Popular designs of plants, animals, and various geometric patterns were not only applied to embroidery but also to the products of other arts and crafts, such as pottery or bronze vessels. Prior to the time of the Shang and Zhou Dynasties (*c.* 1600– 221 BC), the patterns in use tended to be abstract and primitive, but compositions became more balanced, neat and symmetrical after the Zhou Dynasty. In the Tang and Song Dynasties (618–907 and 960–1279), more attention was paid to the various design compositions and by the Ming and Qing periods (1368–1911), designs had become more realistic.

Right *Pair of sleevebands depicting women in a garden, 19th century.*

17

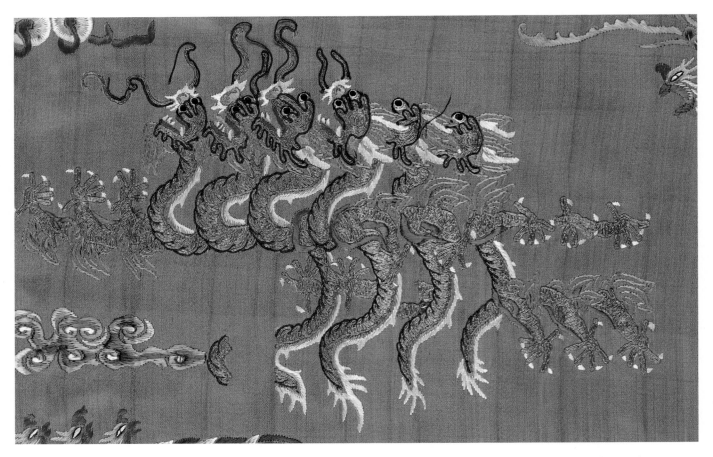

It is not known exactly how designs were transferred, but sometimes lines drawn in ink are to be seen on partly stitched or damaged fragments of antique textiles. Designs were drawn and/or painted first and then transferred to the fabric in marked areas, outlining the shape where the embroidery was required. The fabric was cut and made up into garments or accessories only after the embroidery had been completed. (The Nelson–Atkins Museum in Kansas City, Missouri holds a collection of drawings for embroidery on various robes.)

The discovery of designs with pinholes, from Dunhuang, suggests that the prick-and-pounce method may have been one of the techniques used to transfer designs to fabric. The study of textiles from areas geographically removed from each other suggests that motifs were standardized and constantly repeated.

Books may have been produced holding the various standardized and stylized patterns. Designs on various robes, including imperial robes, jackets and waistcoats, used mirror-image techniques to embroider designs on the front or back pieces of the garments. The same principle was applied to sleevebands found on robes. On pleated items, such as skirts, designs were repeated to accommodate the folding of the fabric.

*Details from a woman's pleated skirt, 19th century. The design, embroidered on green silk fabric, has been broken up and repeated to accommodate the pleats and folds of the skirt. The dragon's scales have been couched with gold threads, and other techniques used in the making of this piece include satin stitch variations. **Above** Design shown with the pleats open. **Right** Another, similar design on the same skirt, shown with the pleats closed.*

The export trade

By the 13th century, Chinese embroidery was being exported to Europe and some samples were used as church vestments. From 1578 the Portuguese were allowed to trade from Canton, and by the 19th century the city had become an important centre for the export of embroidered shawls, hangings, bedcovers, fire screens and so on. Chinese shawls flooded the Spanish markets and though they were copied, brighter colours were used. These copied shawls came to be known as Spanish shawls. Today, sometimes Chinese export shawls are mistaken for or identified as Spanish shawls. These shawls were originally hand-stitched but some of the modern versions are machine-stitched. The coats and jackets made for the European market were embroidered using the same techniques and patterns found in embroideries created for the home market, but were made in a western cut and tended to be overloaded with designs.

In return, Irish linen was exported to China and made into embroidered handkerchiefs. Household articles, such as bedspreads and tablecloths, were made in cotton appliqué. In the mid-19th century, in response to the growing Western interest in antique Chinese textiles, a glut of imitations flooded the market. These imitations were smoked and made to look like old embroideries.

Though many kinds of embroidery techniques are associated with early China, one technique in particular has been described as being Italian in origin, as it looks very similar to the Italian Florentine or Flame stitch, also known as Bargello work, in which subtly varied shades of wool are used to create three-dimensional effects. However, there is no evidence to suggest that the two stitches are directly related.

A variety of embroidery techniques can be found on antique jacket cuffs, insignia badges and skirt panels depicting birds, butterflies or scenes from history,

literature or mythology. Today, many of these antique pieces of Chinese embroidery are available for purchase, either framed as pictures or as collector's pieces. The majority of these date from around the early 18th to late 19th centuries, during the Qing Dynasty period.

Above *This shawl was embroidered in a chinoiserie design that includes ho-ho birds. It was presented to the wife of a cultural attaché at the end of the 19th century and her granddaughter later passed it on to the author.*

Right *A panel of intricate Suzhou embroidery worked in fine threads on a cream silk ground depicting pairs of peacocks, cranes, pheasants, quails and birds of paradise among flowering peonies, prunus and roses. From the Guangxu period (1875–1908). Courtesy of Linda Wrigglesworth.*

Embroidery styles and techniques

Throughout the history of Chinese embroidery, a variety of materials were employed, including woven silk fabrics in plain, satin, damask and fine gauze. Metal threads and paper were used, in addition, of course, to silk threads, either floss or plied in a range of beautifully gradated tones and colours. The combination of these beautiful materials formed an integral part of what has been described as 'painting with the needle', the beautifully realistic style of embroidery, mainly used to depict natural objects and scenes, that has developed over the centuries.

In general, the embroidery was done directly on to the ground fabric, but sometimes it was stitched first on to different silk materials, including gauze and paper. The embroidered pieces were then carefully cut out and applied to another base fabric, either with glue or stitches. This method of applying, stitching and pasting the embroidery created sharp, crisp edges and also helped to stabilize the embroidery stitches.

According to the Chinese, embroidery may be separated into two distinct elements, the *chih wen* and the *tuan chen*. The *chih wen* consists of satin stitch and its variations. The *tuan chen* consists of the Pekin knot and its variations, which were predominantly used in Beijing.

The basic stitches used in embroidery vary according to the different styles, methods of work and areas of China from which any specific embroidery originates. The four main distinct styles of embroidery are known as Su, Xiang, Shu and Yue embroidery, according to the area from which they emerged.

Su embroidery

The style known as Su embroidery originates from the town of Suzhou in the Jiangsu Province, in the east of China. This style of work has a history spanning some

Above *Embroidery of a peony in the Su style. The flowers are depicted as realistically as possible. Courtesy of Alan McIntyre.*

2,000 years and was most highly prized at the Imperial court. The style is famous for its elegant and delicate workmanship, combined with beautiful designs and tasteful, subtle colours. The Su embroidery colour palette contains some 750–1,000 hues, and threads are sometimes dyed to specification for a project.

The stitches used in the Su embroidery style have been classified into nine categories, with some 40 variations of the basic stitches. The following is an extract of notes, provided by my embroidery teacher, and as the English equivalent is the closest translation that I could decipher, any anomalies are my own.

Chinese stitches	English equivalent
Satin stitch	Satin stitch and its variations, such as long and short, encroaching or fishbone stitches
Stitches in disorder	Scatter stitch, random stitch
Needleloop embroidery	Herringbone stitch, detached herringbone stitch
Stripe stitch	Stitches used for lines, such as chain, back, stem and split stitches
Gauze embroidery	Counted thread stitches
Xi embroidery	Overlaid stitches and honeycomb filling
Spot stitch	Pekin knot – used both as seed stitches and solid stitches
Gold thread stitch	Goldwork – couching single or double metal threads
Supplementary stitch	My understanding of this category is that it consists of stitches used to supplement other embroidery techniques.

Right *Shu embroidery peacock from Sichuan province. Courtesy of Alan McIntyre.*

Xiang embroidery

This style has its roots in the folk embroidery of Hunan, where its history goes back some 2,500 years. Archaeological finds excavated in the Changsha area in 1972 have made it possible to trace the progression and development of Xiang embroidery to the Western Han Dynasty (206 BC–8 AD).

Xiang embroidery has been described as featuring bright colours with subtle shadings, having as it does a colour palette consisting of over 100 shades of thread and employing at least 70 types of stitches. The famous Hunan landscape, flower and bird designs were embroidered to imitate nature. Animal subjects are also depicted in as lifelike a manner as possible to display their lustrous, fluffy and furry effects. The fabrics popularly used with this technique include silk damask, transparent gauze and nylon, which is mainly used to create double-sided effects (see page 40). Among the items that are typically decorated with embroidered designs are bedspreads, cushions, pictures, screens, tablecloths and a wide range of different embroidered clothes – for example jackets, trousers and skirts.

Shu embroidery

This embroidery style, also known as Chuan embroidery, is from the Sichuan area and gained prominence during the Qing period. Among the places associated with this style of embroidery are Chongqing, Chengdu, Wenjiang and Beixian in the west of China. Two famous areas in Chengdu, known as Kowloon Alley and Kejia Alley, were once crowded with embroidery workshops set up to produce a variety of items unique to the region. One of the methods of work included in the Shu embroidery stitch vocabulary is the double-sided embroidery technique. The Shu stitch vocabulary extended to some 100 techniques and the types of fabric used included damask and Shu brocade, also made in the area.

Yue embroidery

Also referred to as Guang embroidery, this style is associated with the Canton area, Guandong province. Its origin lay with the minority people of the region and the style became quite popular during the late Ming Dynasty. The work is distinguished by five distinct characteristics, as listed below.

1. The use of a variety of threads, including horsetail hair
2. Strong and bright contrasting colours
3. Extensive use of gold threads to outline designs and patterns
4. Elaborate, rich, colourful and complicated designs
5. Production of the work by men

Other traditional styles

Other styles of embroidery that should be mentioned include Shidao embroidery, which hails from the Shandong province. This type of work, associated with folk art, gained prominence during the Sui and Tang Dynasties (581–907 AD). Its unique artistic style is described as a combination of design and patterns found in Oriental art and the best of Western paintings.

Another type is the folk art embroidery of the Miao minority group from Guizhou province, a style renowned for its use of bright and vivid colours. Woollen needlepoint, cross stitch, cotton embroidery and gold and silver metal thread embroidery techniques are commonly used in this style. Among the popular stitches used is the long-tailed knot, the stitches being worked in abundance to build up a multitude of patterns on the ground fabric.

Above *This 20th-century embroidery of a peacock is worked in bright colours in the Yue style of embroidery from Canton. Courtesy of Alan McIntyre.*
Opposite page *Detail of Miao embroidery from Guizhou province. Courtesy of Gina Corrigan.*

Chinese embroidery through the dynasties

Through the centuries and dynastic reigns, the various styles and techniques of traditional Chinese embroidery have been developed and improved upon. Many examples that have survived can be seen on items of clothing and other decorative ornaments to be found in museums and private collections around the world.

The general style of Chinese embroidery has been described as 'painting with the needle', and the technique involves the use of a variety of stitches including satin stitch, knots, line and other stitches to reproduce realistic designs. The difference between Chinese embroidery and other similar styles lies not only in the fineness of the silk thread that is used but also in the subtly gradated tones and shades of the Chinese colour palette.

The following is a brief summary and breakdown of the embroidery styles and costume designs, including stitches and stitch patterns, that evolved through some of the Chinese dynasties.

Shang Dynasty (c.1600–1027 BC)

Archaeological finds have established that embroidery was first produced during this period, which is also associated with the development of the Chinese dress system.

Han Dynasties (206 BC–AD 220)

This is considered as one of the most important periods with regard to the development and production of silk, the main centres of textile manufacture being set up in Hunan and Shantung provinces. It is also reported that 'three official agencies were set to supervise the production of Imperial robes'. The types of fabrics that were manufactured and popular at that time were plain weave tabby, and plain and patterned gauze weave, which was used as a lightweight fabric during the summer. Han silk was exported through the Silk Road to Palmyra,

Antioch and Rome. Vegetable dyes were used in conjunction with mineral dyes, with some twenty basic colours and several tones and shades.

Designs and motifs included abstract geometric forms, cloud-scrolls patterns, motifs of long life, flowers and birds, landscapes and mythological creatures, to name but a few examples. There is evidence of fabric printing using stencils and block designs, and the use of gold and silver pigments and painted silks.

Subsequently, owing to the economic prosperity of the time, embroidery became widespread. Several variations of chain stitch were very popular and were used in daily life on items of clothing. Braided chain stitch, for example, was an extremely popular version of the basic stitch and was widely used during this period. Embroidery that covered entire areas of the fabric was confined to the narrow borders of cuffs and collars of garments. This trend was popular from the late Shang to the Western Han dynasties.

In AD 59 Emperor Xiaoming instigated costume regulations for court and ritual ceremonies. Strict rules were prescribed for the wearing of a variety of garments and accessories, especially ribbons. The ribbons worn by the emperor and his subordinates were an indication of rank and status. As such, the rules relating to the colours, size and texture of these silk ribbons had to be strictly observed.

Northern and Southern Dynasties (420–580 AD)

Chain stitch remained very popular, but now in some cases the embroidery covered the entire surface of the fabric. Embroidery embellished hangings, altar frontals and banners as well as furniture accessories. Dresses for the aristocracy and furnishing silks were embroidered with motifs such as the endless knot, the lotus flower and the carp. This period also saw the first appearance of beaded circular medallions.

Tang Dynasty (618–907 AD)

The Tang Dynasty presided over one of the most thriving cultures of Chinese history, and while travellers and merchants added to the prosperity and cultural diversity of the period, the development of embroidery styles and techniques progressed rapidly.

After 1,000 years, the predominance of chain stitch was superseded by that of satin stitch and the Pekin knot. These stitches helped to create new visual effects, as diverse stitching variations were created, improved upon and applied. Other methods of work that were developed during the period included the use of shorter stitches covering the entire fabric, appliqué, split stitch and embellishment with beadwork and genuine, highly expensive gold and silver metal threads.

Embroidered articles were given as gifts by emperors to favourite subjects and these were deemed to be especially precious. According to a legend of the time, the first ruling empress of China, Wu Zetian (690–705 AD) presented her prime minister with a fabulous, expensive embroidered robe depicting twelve Chinese characters in gold metal threads.

Embroidery was not only used to decorate a variety of practical articles made at that time, including dresses, bed curtains, quilts and other everyday items, but also for religious purposes, in particular, to embroider pictures of Buddha. Embroidery had long been used for practical and decorative purposes, but the new religious significance that it assumed during the Tang period was due to Buddhist monks. They considered embroidery to be a symbol of honour and diligence, and it was therefore the favourite medium chosen by the monks to create the large-scale portraits of Buddha that were heavily in demand at that time.

One of the many embroidered pictures of Buddha from that period has been described as having elegant and exquisite colouring. The stitching is considered to be even, thin and smooth as if it had been applied with a writing brush. The finished image is comparable to the famous frescoes found in the Dunhuang caves.

During this era a popular design, known as the 'Tang grass design', had evolved from the twisted honeysuckle branch and twisted grass motifs. Another design commonly found during this period was the 'circlet of pearls', which had been imported from the Sassanian (Persian) Empire.

Liao and Song Dynasties (907–1279 AD)

During the Liao and Song periods, at which time painting was the dominant art, the development of embroidery followed a new direction, with actual paintings and painting styles being copied in stitch. Embroidery was worked over a sketch that indicated the important aspect of the subject. Hence, the role of the embroiderer was to supply the details as the work progressed, by choosing the silks and the stitches that were to be used. The ground fabric that was used at that time for silk painting was tabby silk and therefore the same fabric was used for embroidery. The type of embroidery produced was described as being close to the art form used on scrolls, albums and fan leaves.

During the Song Dynasty, under the patronage of Emperor Shen-tsung, in 1063, the Bureau of Fine Textiles (also referred to as the Bureau of Refined Embroideries) at Chengdu, which had long ceased to exist, was reactivated. It brought together famous embroiderers and makers of fine textiles from the whole country. The *chih-kuan-chih* section of the writings of Song history notes that:

The Bureau of Refined Embroideries was in charge of weaving and embroidery for use on carriages, and as regalia and for use in sacrifices made by honoured guests. Over 300 embroiderers were brought into the Bureau.

The importance of embroidery in particular was shown when Emperor Huizong, who reigned between 1101 and 1126, established the Bureau of Embroideries, whose sole task was to produce embroideries, first for the aristocracy and then for the rest of the male population. The emperor was also responsible for setting up a specialized section devoted to embroidered paintings, which were classified into specific categories, such as landscapes, buildings, figures, flowers and birds.

In 1129, the Emperor Gaozong set up a Bureau of Fine Textiles in Hangzhou, the Southern Song capital, as both embroidery and tapestry were greatly appreciated art forms.

Song embroidery was known to be elegant, subtle, restrained but decorative. Dong Qi-chang (1555–1636), a famous Ming critic, described Song embroidery:

> … the stitchery … is fine and tight. Floss is used so that no more than 1 or 2 strands … per inch and the needlework is as fine as human hair. The colouring is marvellous in an ingeniously fine manner, its splendour quite dazzling to the eye. Landscapes distinguish the qualities of the distant and the near; birds capture extremely well the attitude of mildness or rapacity. The finest ones are even better than painting.

Promoted and encouraged by the Imperial court, embroidery developed during the Song period as an art form rather than merely a decorative craft. Embroidery techniques and variations of satin stitch were produced and perfected. Fine needles were used and threads consisting of one to two fine stranded filaments were available in an array of beautiful shaded colours that produced exquisite and delicate work. Geometric and intricate designs, such as the eight trigrams, were popular during that time.

Emperor Huizong, who was himself an artist, founded the Imperial Art Academy, where famous artists of the time gathered and the art of painting flourished. It was in this era that the art of painting and calligraphy merged with the art of embroidery. Embroiderers copied paintings and calligraphy by famous painters and some of the fine embroidery subsequently termed 'embroidery of the inner chambers' was described as being lifelike, with fine and close needlework. (The term 'inner chamber' has been translated approximately to describe the room found on the second floor in traditional large homes of wealthy Chinese families. This area was reserved for the sole use of women of the family, in particular unmarried daughters.)

The flower-painting style of the Academy influenced woven goods and gave rise to realistic styles of design. One of these, known as the 'Lingyang style', was named after the great painter Dou Shihin. Metal threads were popular, and favoured motifs included paired turtledoves, flying rams, soaring phoenixes, swimming fishes and heavenly horses.

Yuan Dynasty (1279–1368)

The Yuan Dynasty was Mongol in origin, and under the leadership of the Emperor Kublai Khan, cultural exchanges were promoted between East and West through the Silk Road.

The Yuan style of embroidery, judging from the few samples of embroidery from this period to have survived, can be described as following in the tradition of the Song style. Coarser velvet and gold brocade were favoured as ground fabric, and the embroidery has been described as rough in style in comparison with the masterful skill of the Song Dynasty embroiderers. The embroidery floss appears to have been rougher and the stitches produced were not so tight. Ink was sometimes used instead of embroidery to paint the eyebrows and the eyes. Metal threads, used extensively during this period to enrich designs, subsequently became influential in the development of the Ming and Qing styles of embroidery.

Ming Dynasty (1368–1644)

During the Ming Dynasty, the decorative aspects of embroidery were revived under the Imperial tutelage, and followed the Song style of embroidery. At this time, embroidery was popular among people from widely different social classes, being used for a multitude of purposes. Satin stitch was applied in all its variations in conjunction with seed stitch and stem stitch, thus providing a varied combination of techniques. This era also saw the development of hair embroidery, with human hair being used instead of silk threads. This type of embroidery, worked on satin silk fabric, followed painting techniques, as the needles threaded with hair were used to imitate pen-and-ink drawing techniques.

The use of gold and other metal threads in embroidery was a common feature of the Ming style. The gold threads were made of thin strips of gold leaf wrapped around fine red silk. Other types of embroidery that developed at this time included flannel embroidery and lace embroidery. As Ming sumptuary laws circumscribed the use of gold, couched, wrapped gold threads were used on Imperial objects only, with gold outlines being prescribed for people of lesser importance.

Though more lustrous colours were available and the work has been described as being far richer in texture and colour, the Ming Dynasty style of work is considered to be less delicate than the more elegant work undertaken during the Song Dynasty.

Above *The eight trigrams, a motif popular during the Song Dynasty. This shape was regularly used as a base for the embroidered medallions that are found on sleeveband designs, decorated with either scenery or symbolic motifs.*

Gu embroidery

The Ming Dynasty also saw the development of the Gu style of embroidery. The technique used painting to replace some areas of stitching, and threads in a variety of rich colours were applied for layering and shading, thus creating harmonious embroideries. In this endeavour, the Ming ladies broke with tradition and included materials other than silk. New materials included human and animal hairs, and feathers and fur were also added to give realistic proportions to the designs.

Gu embroidery was modelled on famous landscape, bird and flower paintings, and portrayals of immortals and human figures, all taken from masterpieces of the Song and Yuan dynasties. In particular, it was greatly influenced by the style of painting of the Ming Dynasty's Songjiang circle of painters, known among the elite as the Clouds Clique (*Don Su Chan*).

The name of this technique was taken from the Gu family of Shanghai (1556) which became renowned because of the imperial candidate Gu Mingshi. He lived in Luxiangyuan in the Jiumu district and this embroidery was also known as the Luxiangyuan embroidery. Han Xi-meng, the wife of Gu Shou-chien, second grandson of Gu Mingshi, was the embroiderer who not only perfected the technique but also is one of the few women in Chinese history to be properly acknowledged for her embroidery skills.

Han Xi-meng was a skilled painter, especially of plants, and her work reflected her mastery of the theory of painting in addition to her fine embroidery skills. She was also ingenious in her original use of colour. This talented woman became the most prominent female embroiderer of her day, and her work has been referred to as the 'embroidery of the woman Han' or 'Miss Han embroidery'.

The Gu family of embroiderers believed that 'nothing was impossible in needlework and that when an embroidery looked like a painting, then nothing more remained to be done'. The term 'Gu family embroidery' was also applied to the work of other members of the Gu household, including Miss Han's granddaughter, two maids-in-waiting to the Gu household, T'ai-hsueh and Gu Yen-p'ing, and the concubine Lan-yu, and later the term referred to any embroiderer who copied their style. A skilled embroiderer was known at the time as *qiao shou*, a 'clever hand' or *neng shou,* a 'capable hand'.

The Gu technique has been described as combining at least 10 different types of stitches and several methods of application. These include satin shading, applied using single, double and multiple layer techniques, for example block shading (*qiang* method) close knit stitches (*shan tao* and *ping tao* methods) and carved scale stitch methods. Other commonly used stitches were split stitch, knot stitch and couching with metal threads, to name but a few.

Silk floss threads incorporated a variety of lightly or tightly twisted filaments that were sometimes blended, wound and plied with feathers, especially those of the Siamese fighting cock, to produce interesting rough textures. Hair was used to re-create lifelike effects.

There are some 32 items displaying the Gu style of embroidery in the Liaoning Provincial Museum. Other examples are to be found in the museums of Shanghai, Nanjing, Suzhou and Zhenjiang.

Also during the Ming period, the rules and regulations pertaining to the dress code that had been established during the Yuan Dynasty were abolished. Reforms to the new dress code reflected native traditions rooted in Han, Tang and Song cultures, the revised laws for clothing being determined in 1391 and finally codified in 1587.

Qing Dynasty (1644–1911)

The Manchus who set up the Qing Dynasty were horse-riding nomads from the north and related to the reigning Mongols of the Yuan Dynasty. Their tastes have been described as more forthright and less subtle than those of the Yuan Dynasty, and one of their innovations was the dragon robe. Known as *chi fu* in Chinese, and literally translated as Manchu robe, the dragon robe was designed as formal wear. The design was a combination of the ancient silk-embroidered robe traditional to the indigenous Han Chinese and the close-cut, horse-riding skin coat worn by the nomadic warriors from the steppes who invaded Manchuria in 1644. Slight changes in the colour and rendering of various details indicate the chronology of these robes through various dynastic reigns. The wearing of these robes and other items of court costume was rigidly controlled by statutory laws set up by the Manchus and provided an indication of the wearer's place in the hierarchical Qing Dynasty. In general, clothing fell into official and non-official categories, which were further broken down into formal, semi-formal and informal groups.

The Qing dynasty came to an end in 1911. The life story of its last emperor, Pu-yi, was made into a film, *The Last Emperor*, in 1987, directed by Bernardo Bertolucci.

Right *Jacket and trousers, late 19th–early 20th century. Although these two items have been paired, they are not from the same period or area. The jacket, made of red silk damask, is embroidered only around the sleeves and neck, in subtle shades reminiscent of the 'famille verte' palette found on Chinese porcelain and dates from around 1870. The trousers are made from gauze and were worn in summer. The edges of the trouser legs are embroidered in blue cross stitch. Above this blue border, a coarser and brighter design of flowers and fruits, embroidered in Pekin knot, has been appliquéd.*

Dragon robes

The dragon robes that were worn by the emperor and his officials on the most formal occasions were decorated with a depiction of the universe and dragons. In addition to their purely decorative usage, they carried figurative symbolic meanings through their designs and embroidery. The dragon robe worn by the emperor, for example, carried twelve symbols reserved specially for him. The breakdown of the symbols and their meanings are set out in the Symbols section (see page 104).

The dragon design

This became the symbol of supreme, supernatural power. On robes from the Qing Dynasty, two small five-clawed dragons were used to symbolize the emperor's power of adaptability through renewal or transformation, as the dragon was deemed to have the gift of making itself visible or invisible. When the dragon was combined with the axe, the *fu* symbol (see page 107) and the pheasant, it implied the judicial powers of the court. The dominant image on semi-formal or informal robes of the Qing period is that of a dragon playing with either a pearl, a flaming disc or an orb. The pearl is believed to represent the pearl of wisdom, a symbol of the emperor's search for virtue on behalf of the empire.

The five-clawed dragon (*lung*) was reserved to be worn by the emperor and his immediate family – his sons and princes of the first and second ranks. Princes of the third and fourth ranks wore the four-clawed dragon (*mang*). During the Tang Dynasty a three-clawed dragon had been used until the five-clawed dragon replaced it.

The decoration on the upper part of the Imperial ritual robe suggests the sky. At the bottom of the robe, the large oblique lines represent the ocean, with waves and spray *(li shui)* breaking at the foot of mountains, usually represented by four rocks – a symbol of the four cardinal points.

This section of the design also symbolized the forces of nature. The height of the *li shui* border gained importance during the 18th century, and by the 19th it had increased to such an extent that this area could fill at least a quarter of the robe. This fact is useful, as it helps to identify the period of a garment. All the symbolic meanings attached to these official garments came into full force when worn by the emperor and his officials during ceremonies.

Though informal robes were also embroidered with symbols, including flowers and birds, they were less ornate that those worn by the emperor and his family. The colour yellow, also termed imperial yellow, was reserved solely for his use and that of close members of his family. In general, men wore black, dark blue and purple, while women favoured pink and green. Red was a colour of joy, while dull grey and white were for mourning.

Accessories were elaborately decorated, not only with embroidery, but also with precious stones and feathers. Decorative items of this type included badges of rank, purses, hats, cloud collars, waistcoats, fan holders, mirror holders and shoes.

Above *Detail from a li shui border, embroidered in a variety of satin stitches. Auspicious symbols have been placed among the waves and spray. Courtesy of Meg Andrews.*

Above *A pair of 19th-century circular badges with five-clawed dragons finely embroidered with gold threads. Courtesy of Meg Andrews.*

Footwear

The two main styles of shoes for men were made of plain black satin, cotton or velvet fabrics with stiff and thick soles. The soles, measuring 3–7 centimetres (1–3 inches) thick, were made with either layers of paper or old rags. As they were flat and rigid, they were made shorter than the uppers in order to facilitate walking. The plain fabrics were sometimes decorated with stitch and appliqué. Black satin boots were also worn by men.

Shoes for women could be placed into two main categories, described as *lotus* and *platform*. The lotus shoes worn by Han Chinese women with bound feet (a custom abolished in 1912) were so named because the ladies who wore them were described as swaying elegantly like a lotus in the wind. To imitate the sway of the lotus, Manchu women, who did not have bound feet, wore shoes raised on to platforms. The styles for bound feet were regional, such as the Shanghai style, which had undulating soles, the Beijing style with leather soles and reinforced heels, or the style from South China with flat heels. Most shoes were exquisitely decorated with embroidery, appliqué, beads and other methods of work. To show her needlework dexterity, the young Han woman produced between three and 16 pairs of lotus shoes as part of her dowry. The Manchu shoes known as 'platform' or 'boat' shoes also had heels in a variety of styles.

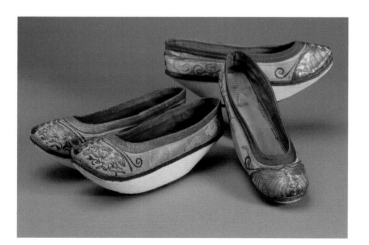

Left *Manchu 'boat' shoes. Courtesy of Linda Wrigglesworth.* **Above** *Manchu shoe, made for a young girl from fine gauze embroidered in pink and blue.* **Below** *Drawing of a Manchu platform shoe.* **Above right** *Lotus shoes made for the 20th-century tourist market from 19th-century embroidered fabrics.* **Below right** *lotus shoes, middle to late 19th century, with embroidered and appliquéd soles.*

Mandarin squares or badges of rank

A simple dark coat, called a *pu-fu*, worn over the dragon robe and by officials on ceremonial occasions, carried a badge of rank – either square or circular in shape – at the centre back and front of the garment. The front badge was split in two for the opening. These insignia were used to denote rank; the shape of the circular badges being a reference to the shape of heaven, they thus took precedence over square badges. Worn shortly after the founding of the Ming Dynasty (1368–1644) until the fall of the Qing Dynasty in 1911, these badges may possibly be the first of the name or identification badges that are so commonly used nowadays.

The badges of rank were broken down in two distinct sets. The first represented the civil mandarins, who were highly respected scholars who administered the government. Their appointment to office was through a series of tough examinations. The second set represented the military officials, chosen more for their bravery, prowess with weapons or through family connections than through success in formal examinations. Their responsibility was to defend the country and keep the peace. Each set of badges was divided into nine elements and sub-divided into a principal and secondary order. The civil officials' badges carried depictions of birds, while the military badges displayed real and mythical animals.

Before the 19th century, the various animals depicted on military badges were generally shown looking towards a red disc on the left, which represented the sun, while the birds depicted on civil officials' badges were shown with spread wings and turning to face the sun on the right. However, bird designs appeared during the 19th century with the sun disc on the left-hand corner and animals depicted facing to the right.

Badges were either woven, using a method known as *kesi,* or embroidered. Designs were generally set in clouds and sea, and the wide range of stitches used included satin stitch, surface stitch, raised stitch, vine tendrils, fern stitch, long and short, couching, laid work, knots, split stitch, pattern darning, counted stitch on gauze and goldwork.

Civil officials' insignia

1. Manchurian crane
2. Golden pheasant
3. Peacock
4. Wild goose
5. Silver pheasant
6. Egret
7. Mandarin duck
8. Quail
9. Paradise flycatcher

Military officials' insignia

1. *Qi lin* (mythical animal)
2. Lion *(shi zi)*
3. Leopard
4. Tiger
5. Bear
6. Panther *(biao)*
7. Rhinoceros *(xi niu)*
8. Rhinoceros *(xi niu)*
9. Sea horse *(hai ma)*

Top left *Qi Lin, first military rank. This badge was made for the export market and dates from around 1900. The couched gold threads around the border have been added at a later date, probably during the last 20 years.* Top right *Manchurian crane, first civil rank. Also made for export, this badge depicts a Manchurian crane amid spray and waves, with flowers and four bats.* Bottom *Egret, sixth civil rank. This badge appears to be an original, dating from the late 18th or early 19th centuries. An egret with spread wings, facing the solar disc, is embroidered with goldwork, surrounded by a border of stylized* shou *good-luck characters.*

Embroidery from the past to the present

During the Qing period (1644–1911), regional and other individual embroidery styles were developed further, each one gaining more prominence in its own right, and they have all continued to flourish separately from one another.

In today's China, the provinces of Jiangsu, Hunan, Sichuan and Guandong, each of which have developed their own highly reputable styles of embroidery, known as Su, Xiang, Shu and Yue respectively, remain the main centres for embroidery in China. The work produced in each of these areas is still prized for its great beauty, intricate detail and skilful workmanship.

One of the most famous and leading exponents of

embroidery in the modern era was Shen Shou (1874–1921), who taught at the Imperial embroidery workshop in Beijing. She had trained as an artist in fine arts and her embroidery has been described as fine art embroidery. Another embroiderer, Yang Shouyu (1896–1981), developed the style of random stitch embroidery. Both Shen Shou and Yang Shouyu are responsible for the development of Suzhou embroidery today through the Suzhou Embroidery Research Institute (SERI).

New techniques are developed and are added to the old styles, and there is continual research into embroidery technology. Among those developed techniques are new forms of hair embroidery,

double-sided embroidery and double-faced embroidery. Chinese embroidery is enjoying a revival, and visitors to the main four areas named above may find a multitude of traditional designs or modern pieces of embroidery for sale in local shops.

The only hair embroidery research centre in the world is the Wenzhou Portrait Embroidery Institute, which specializes in exploring modern portraits embroidered with hair. The styles used at the institute are divided into colour embroidery, sketch embroidery and hair embroidery. Sketch embroidery uses only one shade of silk thread but different hues to create depth to a portrait. Professor Wei Jinxian is one of the leading exponents of hair embroidery.

Above *Detail of a peony embroidered in the Su style, showing the intricate colour shading used to represent the velvety petals. Courtesy of Alan McIntyre.*

Left *Suzhou garden scenery, 20th century. This picture is an example of the style of embroidery that is being produced for the tourist market today. It is possibly based on a scene from the picturesque Master of the Nets garden in Suzhou. Old satin stitch techniques have been merged with new random-style techniques, which are used extensively to depict scenery. Courtesy of Alan McIntyre.*

Double-sided embroidery

As its name suggests, works produced using this technique are exactly the same on each side.

The silk threads used for double-sided embroidery may be split into extremely fine filaments, comparable to one quarter of the diameter of a single strand of hair. The ends of the threads, which are hidden on the opposite face of the embroidery, appear as tiny dots that measure less than one fifth of a millimetre. As these dots are barely visible to the naked eye, it is therefore possible to conceal the ends and joints within an embroidered design. A particularly difficult subject to embroider using the double-sided technique is fish, as the embroiderer aims to reproduce the lifelike qualities of translucency and movement. To embroider a fish's tail is a time-consuming affair, as the shorter and finer filaments that must be used have a tendency to break easily.

Above *Cat, 20th century. Animal pictures are a favourite with the Western visitor to China and these cats can be found in a multitude of poses and colours, embroidered mainly for the tourist market. The embroidery is generally double-sided and directional stitches are used to portray the fur. Different levels of quality and finish, from mediocre to exquisite, can now be purchased.*

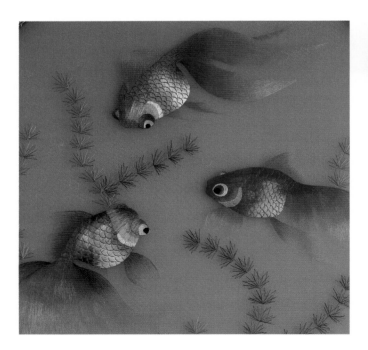

Left *This double-sided piece of embroidery uses filaments that are so fine they appear to be translucent. Very fine examples like this tend to be more expensive than other double-sided pictures because they can take up to a year to embroider.*

Double-faced embroidery

Though double-sided embroidery had long been in use in the past, a new development based on its reversible technique was invented by Miss Peng Jianchun in 1979, and developed further in the 1980s by the Hunan Embroidery Research Institute. In this technique, referred to as 'double-faced' or 'discrepant' embroidery, the design embroidered on one side of the fabric may be different to that on the other side, despite having been stitched simultaneously, or the same design may be worked on either side of the fabric, but incorporating a different colour combination, as in the example below. Another name that is sometimes used to describe this technique is 'double-sided three-difference' embroidery.

Double-faced embroidery is more complicated to stitch than double-sided embroidery. It requires the embroiderer to work on the two faces of a base material simultaneously, creating an entirely different embroidered subject on each side of the fabric. The secret of double-faced embroidery lies in the meticulous concealment of the threads. To manipulate the needles for this technique, a high degree of skilled craftsmanship and dexterity are required. The use of perspective study, a knowledge of anatomy and an innate sense of colour are important – indeed essential – factors that enable the embroiderer to accommodate the variety of shaping and modelling processes that are encountered using this technique.

The ultra-fine silk threads used in double-faced embroidery are the same as those required for double-sided embroidery. Typical designs might depict a monkey on one side and a tiger on the other, a lady warrior on one side and a woman of peace on the other, or perhaps a cat on one side and a dog on the other. Figurative couples may also be embroidered, with the man on one side and the woman on the other.

Right and far right *Double-faced picture of a cat playing with a grasshopper, showing two sides of the same embroidery. Such effects involve remarkable skill and artistry. However, this is a fairly basic use of the technique in comparison with some of the more intricate double-faced designs that are currently available.*

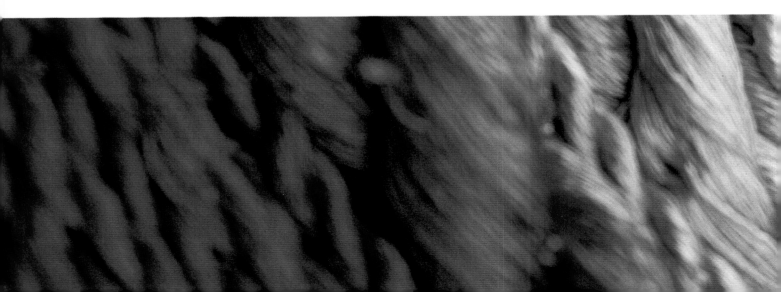

Chapter Two
Materials and basic techniques

Frames, fabrics, needles and threads

Frames

For successful results, it is essential that the fabric is mounted tautly on a frame, and to achieve the correct tension, the fabric has to be laced. Traditional frames are rectangular in shape and are designed to hold the fabric taut for embroidery. Although I normally work on a traditional Chinese frame, it is possible to use any of the free-handed frames that are available in the shops.

Fabrics

For my embroidery sessions in China, I was provided with a medium-weight Habotai silk upon which to embroider. A wide range of silk fabrics is suitable, however, and the huge variety of silk fabrics that are available today provides embroiderers with a vast array from which to choose. The only criterion is that the chosen fabric must be able to sustain the weight of the embroidery. For this reason, it is advisable to use a medium-to-heavy silk, such as a damask, twill, silk satin, plain weave silk or even a patterned silk brocade. My personal choice of fabric for Chinese embroidery is duchesse silk satin, in either white or cream. As an alternative to silk, man-made fabrics, such as plain or dyed polyester satin or nylon, may be used for embroidery.

Needles

The earliest needles were made of bone or ivory, after which came copper, bronze and steel. Nowadays, quilting needles sizes 9, 10 and 12 or Sharps No. 12 may be used for Chinese embroidery. Hand-made steel needles approximately 26mm (1 inch) in length, and in degrees of thickness ranging from fine to heavy, can be purchased from specialist suppliers.

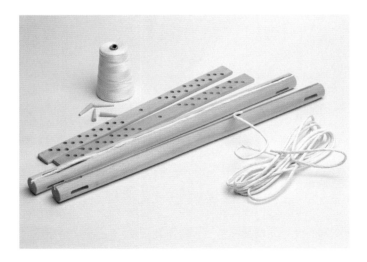

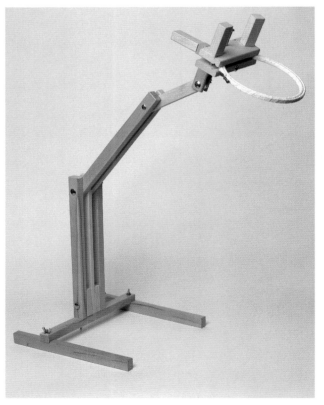

Above *A modern adaptation of the traditional Chinese embroidery frame, shown dismantled. It consists of two vertical bars with holes (which can be used for lacing), two horizontal bars with grooves to use for holding the fabric with paper cord, and pegs for tensioning and holding the frame. Courtesy of BWH Designs.* **Right** *Stand with circular frame. Courtesy of Whitmac Designs.*

Transferring designs on to fabric

There are several methods that can be used to transfer designs on to fabric and they can be found in general craft and textile books. Some of the methods that may be adapted for use in Chinese embroidery are listed below.

Paint and brush method

One of the traditional methods used in China is the application of watercolour paint with a paintbrush. An artist will draw his original design freehand on to the fabric once it has been mounted. Black paint is usually applied on white or other light-coloured fabrics and white paint is used on transparent and dark fabrics. The paint must be reapplied once the lines fade.

Above *This work in progress is stitched on nylon fabric in Chinese silk threads. The design outline is transferred using white watercolour paint and a brush and has to be reapplied when the lines fade.*

Tracing paper method

Another method uses tracing paper, on to which the design is marked in pencil. Four magnets or masking tape can be used to hold the design in place on the reverse side of the fabric. Then a B or H pencil is used to transfer the design on to the fabric. A lightbox or daylight through a window can accentuate the view of the design outline.

Tissue paper method

In this method, the design is traced on to tissue paper or stitch-and-tear paper, which is secured to the fabric with a few stitches at each corner. The design is transferred by tacking (basting) the outline with running stitch, after which the paper is torn away and removed. Alternatively, split stitch may be used for outlining.

Prick and pounce method

In this traditional method, the design is first transferred on to tracing paper, then placed on an ironing board or piece of polystyrene board and pricked at regular intervals around the outline with a needle. Once placed on to the fabric and secured with either stitch or masking tape, pounce, such as powdered charcoal, can be applied over the holes with a soft brush, using a circular motion. The paper is then gently removed and, with a fine brush, the outline of the design is followed with watercolour paint. When the paint is dry, the excess powder is gently patted out.

Template method

A popular method used in China is the use of templates made out of stiff card. This method allows the same motif to be repeated several times or reversed for a mirror-image effect. Any design or motif can be enlarged or reduced and then transferred as a template. The design is transferred on to tracing paper and secured to the card with masking tape. Then the template is cut out with a craft knife.

Silk threads

For the purposes of this book and ease of identification, I have divided the threads that may be used for Chinese embroidery into four categories.

1. Chinese silk thread and Western equivalents, such as Pearsall's Filoselle silk threads.
2. Flat silk threads as used in oriental embroidery, and other similar silk threads.
3. Commercially plied silk threads, such as Gütermann or Mulberry silk.
4. Metal threads, such as the range available from general and specialist suppliers.

The quality of Chinese silk thread and the range of colours produced depends on the area of origin, as each region tends to promote its local silk industry. The number of filaments contained in each strand of silk can vary between approximately 40 and 80. The silk is softly twisted and is versatile to work with; each strand may be split into finer filaments according to the requirements of the design in hand. This thread is therefore an ideal choice for the fine and subtle double-sided embroidery. The embroiderer can use this type of thread in a variety of ways:

- Remove the soft twist and split the filaments into finer elements.
- Work with the thread as it is or combine two or more strands for a thicker finish.
- Twist the thread in an S or Z twist in a range of thickness, either on its own or plied with other type of threads, such as metal threads or other materials, such as feathers.

Though the threads listed above can be used for any type of embroidery, the first group is better suited for use with satin stitch variations, while the third group is ideal for knot stitches. Metal thread is used as either one strand, for outlining and filling voiding, or two strands, for general metal thread techniques.

Though other types of silk thread, such as those from group 2, can be used in the same way as those from group 1, their individual strands do not lend themselves to being split into finer strands for Chinese embroidery. Therefore a common problem that arises is that the finished work tends to have a 'fluffy' quality.

Colours

The subtle range of colours within the Chinese palette of threads plays an essential role in creating the delicate finish and fine colour shading that is characteristic of the traditional Chinese technique of painting with the needle. When commission work is undertaken, threads are sometimes dyed to specification.

Other threads

Due to the present difficulty of getting hold of the Chinese silk threads, I have tested several alternatives that may be used as a substitute for the authentic Chinese floss. One of those that I have found suitable is the Filoselle range from Pearsall's (see Useful Addresses on page 125). This range is readily available and not only does it contain a good series of subtle colours but the individual strands can be split into fine filaments for Chinese embroidery.

Other types of silk, including Mulberry and Gütermann silks as well as stranded cotton threads, may be substituted and adapted for use with Chinese embroidery. It is important to note, however, that the visual effect of the finished embroidery is dependent on the type of fabric, threads and colours used.

Right *Skeins of Pearsall's Filoselle silk threads in subtle shade variations.*

Splitting threads into finer filaments

There are several methods of splitting silk threads, though the process can be made easier by using a pad, made from either polystyrene or mounting board cut to a size of 20 x 12cm (8 x 5in) and covered in dark-coloured velvet (or light-coloured velvet if you are using dark-coloured thread).

Thread the needle with a manageable strand of thread, around 20–25cm (8–10in) in length. Anchor the thread to the needle, as shown in the diagram on the opposite page, before attempting to split it up into finer elements.

Secure the needle at the top of the velvet pad and smooth the silk thread down the length of the fabric towards the bottom of the pad (see photograph below). The nap of the velvet will catch the silk, making it easier for you to separate the filaments. Using the tip of a tapestry needle, pull the threads apart and break the excess filaments, leaving the required fine floss ready for embroidery. It is advisable to thread several needles with the same fineness of thread you have chosen to work with, and place one of them aside as a reference sample. This will help you to gauge the fineness of thread required for subsequent rows of stitches and other projects.

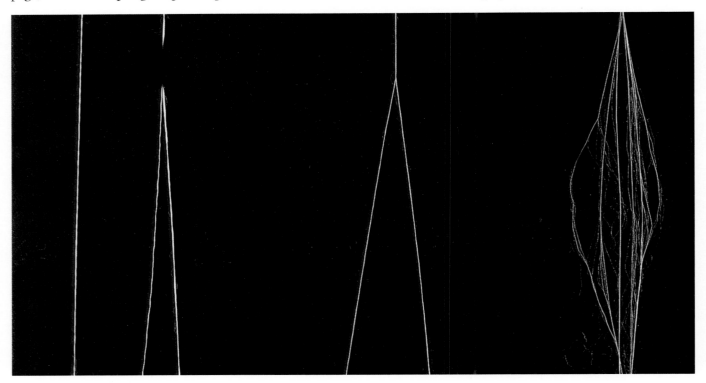

Above *Pearsall's Filoselle silk threads divided into two, then split further into finer filaments.*

Breakdown of single strand of Chinese silk into finer filaments					
1 strand of silk (approx. 48 filaments) split into	2	4	6	8	extremely fine filaments
Approx. number of filaments per split strand	24f	12f	8f	6f	

S twist

clockwise

Z twist

anticlockwise

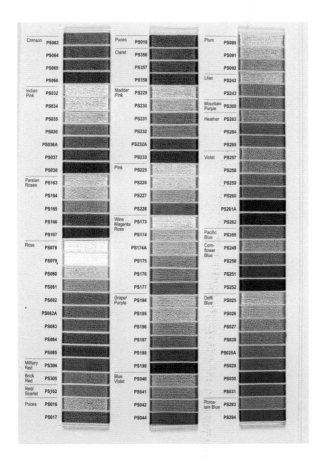

Above *A small selection of the colours available in the Pearsall's Filoselle range.*

Anchoring the thread before starting to ply or stitch

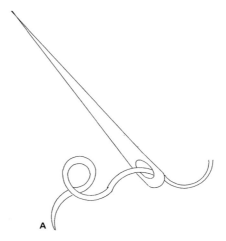

A

Step 1

Hold the end of the thread (A) with the left hand. Hold the needle and the rest of the thread with the right hand. Turn the thread over itself, in an anticlockwise direction.

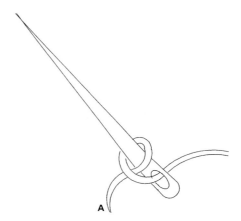

A

Step 2

Place the needle in the loop you have formed. Pull the end of the thread (A) tight to form a knot.

Step 3

Slip the knot to the top end of the needle's eye.

Preparing to stitch

Silk fabrics are often 'weighted' with a chemical preparation to enhance their appearance and feel. To avoid the risk of shrinkage or other problems at a future date, it is a wise precaution to follow the washing and ironing or dry cleaning instructions for the fabric you have selected before preparing it for embroidery.

Requirements

• 30 × 40cm (12 × 16in) of silk fabric suitable for embroidery

• 30cm (12in) of calico or polycotton fabric

• Sewing equipment and sewing machine

• Frame

• Strong threads for lacing

Cut the calico into two strips, each measuring 15 × 30cm (6 × 12in), and machine or hand stitch a strip to opposite sides of the silk fabric, using a French seam. The finished French seam should be on the right side of the fabric. This seam is useful for anchoring the fine needles, threaded or unthreaded, as a substitute for a pincushion.

Make 12mm ($^1/_2$ in) turnings along the remaining raw edges and machine or hand stitch the turnings to prepare the fabric's edge for lacing (see steps 1–3, right). The fabric is now ready to be mounted in the frame.

Once the fabric has been mounted, you can choose a design and select the appropriate colours of thread. To avoid distortion, designs are generally transferred to the fabric after it has been stretched and mounted. Several methods of transfer can be used (see Transferring designs on to fabric, page 45).

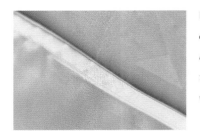

Left *The French seam at the edge of the fabric can be useful for holding fine needles, threaded and unthreaded, when working.*

Preparing the fabric edge for lacing

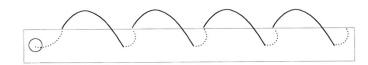

Step 1

Secure the thread on the left or right of the front of the fabric. Bring the needle to the back and stitch the thread to the edge of the fabric in big loops, following the diagram. Space the stitches about 2–3cm ($^3/_4$–$1^1/_4$in) apart.

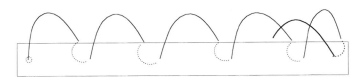

Step 2

Go back up the edge of the fabric, reversing the process.

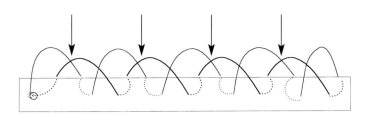

Step 3

The finished fabric edge. The lacing is done through the loops marked with arrows.

Mounting fabric on a frame

The following instructions show the traditional Chinese method of mounting a frame, but the method can be adapted to work with slate and other rectangular frames. The lacing is useful as it allows the frame to be dismantled and reassembled fairly quickly.

Place the fabric and frame on a flat surface. Working with one horizontal bar at a time, place the fabric in the groove and hold in place with paper cord (Chinese embroiderers sometimes use a piece of newspaper with a piece of fabric twisted with an S or Z twist instead of paper cord). Roll the fabric round the bottom bar to within 6-10cm (2¹/₂–4in) of the French seam. (pic 1).

Insert the vertical bars into the grooves on the bottom horizontal bar and adjust to suit the size of the rolled fabric. Place the pegs in the holes and tension temporarily.

Lacing

Cut a piece of string 3-4m 3¹/₄–4¹/₂yd) long and secure one end to the bottom right-hand bar of the frame. Lace the fabric to the vertical bar by catching the edge stitch with the string and wrapping it around the vertical bars, working from the bottom to the top. Secure the threads temporarily but as tightly as possible round the peg at the top (pic 2). Repeat on the other side of the frame.

When both sides of the frame have been laced, adjust the tension by firmly pulling the loops of string (pic 3), working from the bottom to the top, and securing the end of the string tightly to the frame (pic 4). Diagram 5 shows the finished laced frame.

Dismantling and reassembling

To dismantle the frame, undo the string, leaving the lacing in place, and remove the vertical bars. Roll the fabric on to the bottom horizontal bar and put the work away. When you wish to resume work on your embroidery, unroll the fabric from the horizontal bar on which it has been stored and slide the vertical bar back into the loose loops of string (pic 6). Then repeat the lacing process, as detailed above.

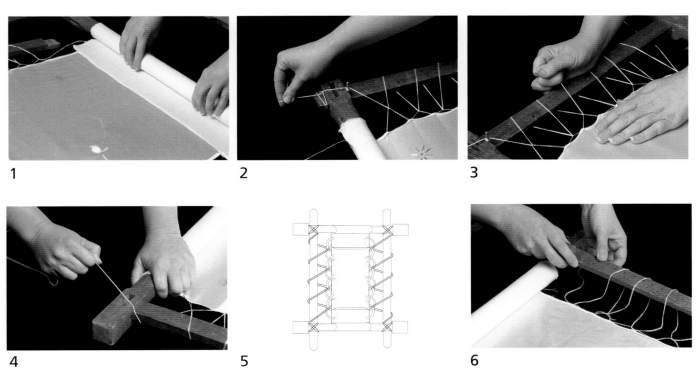

1

2

3

4

5

6

Starting to stitch

When stitching, the right hand stays on top of the fabric to push the needle down. The left hand is placed under the frame on the reverse of the fabric to receive the needle. (This should be reversed for left-handed embroiderers.)

In general, embroidery stitches tend to be worked in a top-to-bottom movement, following the direction of the design, with rows being worked from left to right. There are no hard and fast rules about where stitching should start. Each design, however, has to be assessed and worked individually, and there are times when this basic top-to-bottom, left-to-right process has to be reversed, either to accommodate the embroiderer or the design in hand.

Stitch direction

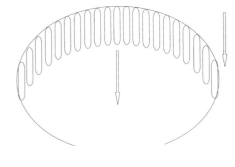

Working direction

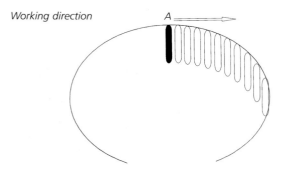

From centre (A) to the right

Edging motifs

Satin stitch is covered at greater length in the following section, but it is worth noting here that sometimes, when individual motifs are embroidered using stitches from that group, they are first outlined either with split stitch, back stitch or stem stitch. This provides a sharp and solid edge to the embroidery.

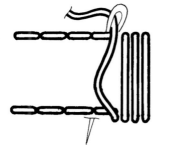

Satin stitch worked over rows of back stitch

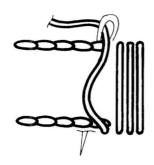

Satin stitch worked over rows of split stitch

Working direction

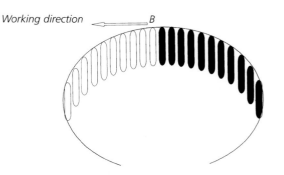

From off-centre (B) to the left

Invisible dot or pinhead

In traditional Chinese embroidery, when working with very fine threads, the thread ends are carefully hidden with invisible dots, to create a neat finish on both the front and back of the work. The invisible dot is worked in an area – within the design but close to the starting point – which will eventually be covered with the embroidery. The invisible dot should be used every time you start or finish with a new piece of thread.

Stitching an invisible dot

Step 1

With the right (or dominant) hand, push the needle through the top of the fabric, close to the spot where work is to begin, within the design area. Pull the needle with the left hand on the reverse of the fabric and under the frame, but hold the last 2.5–5cm (1–2in) of the thread on top with your right thumb. Sometimes it takes several attempts to get started as the top thread tends to slip out of the fabric or the thread slips out of the needle if it is not anchored beforehand, as described on page 49.

Step 2

The needle re-enters from the back, as close as possible to the starting point. This should catch the fabric slightly and, when the needle is reinserted, create a barely visible dot.

Repeat steps 1 and 2 two or three times, or until you feel that the thread is secure and will not pull away. Finishing with the needle on the top of the fabric, pull the thread end that is on the top of the fabric taut and cut it off, as close to the fabric as you can.

Finishing with an invisible dot

Bring the needle up from the back of the fabric and gently push it between the stitches of the work in hand, taking care not to catch any of the top stitches or disturb the embroidery. Work two small invisible dots in the same manner as described in Steps 1 and 2. Finish by bringing the needle and thread back on to the top of the fabric. Pull the thread tight and cut it close to the embroidery, taking care not to damage your work.

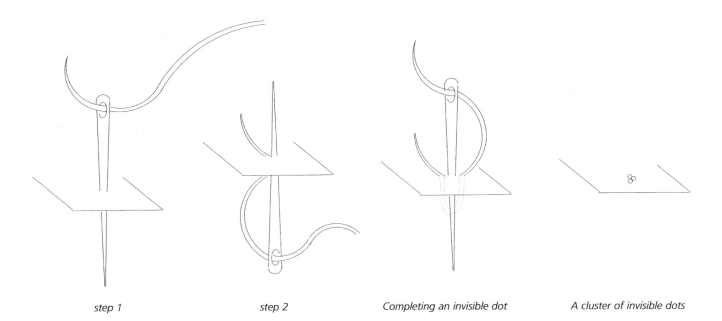

step 1   step 2   Completing an invisible dot   A cluster of invisible dots

Chapter Three
Chinese embroidery stitches

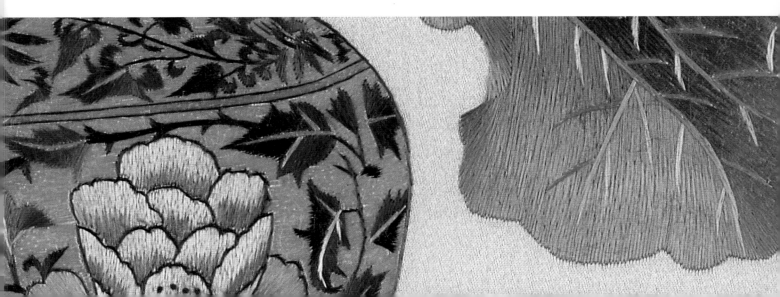

Satin stitch and its variations

The stitches in this group are the most versatile in the repertoire of traditional Chinese embroidery and are used extensively. Referred to as *chih wen* in China, they are broken down into various categories, as the application and method of work are not only dependent on individual designs but also on the area of origin. Some stitches, again according to the area of origin, are specifically named to accommodate a design. For example, to embroider the wing of a butterfly, the stitch technique referred to as 'outward qiang' is applied, while the stitch techniques falling into the group known as 'scale carving' are used to depict the scales of fish and dragons.

Two other techniques that must be mentioned here because they fall into the general category of satin stitch variations are random stitch and colour borrowing.

Random stitch
This is best described as irregular straight stitches arranged at random to build up layers with a multitude of coloured threads. The technique, which has a modern appearance to it, has been added to the traditional stitches and designs that form part of the Suzhou style of embroidery. Random stitch is popularly used to depict masterpieces of classic and modern art.

Colour borrowing
There are several methods of working this technique, which combines embroidery and painting as used in the style of Gu embroidery. It is a time-saving method of work, especially when large embroideries are required. Embroidery is used either to cover the outline or the main part of the design, and paint is subsequently applied to the rest. Sometimes gold leaf is used, either instead of paint or in conjunction with it. Variations of satin stitch shading are used for this technique.

A breakdown of satin stitch and its variations are laid out on the following pages. Within this section I have used the direct English translations of the Chinese names, with the Chinese names themselves in italic where appropriate. Where possible, I have also listed the Western equivalent of the stitches.

Basic satin stitches – horizontal, vertical and diagonal
Another name for satin stitch is even stitch, because the stitches can be arranged in regular flat rows, without overlapping or gaps left between rows of stitching. This stitch can not only be used to embroider a multitude of flora and fauna designs, but can also cover large areas to make a foundation layer on which to superimpose other patterns (see page 75).

The stitches follow the natural direction found in the design being embroidered, and the threads can be laid horizontally, vertically or diagonally at a 45-degree angle. When this is used as a filling stitch, the play of light on the threads adds lustre and shine to the embroidery.

There are two clear methods for applying this stitch. The first uses a full stitch that covers both the front and back of the embroidery. This method requires more thread and therefore tends to be used for smaller designs. The second method, surface stitch, which is normally used for larger pieces of work, is quicker to apply and uses less thread, because the stitch only covers the surface of the fabric.

Open fishbone stitch
A variation that falls under the general category of satin stitch is open fishbone stitch, which is used primarily to embroider branches, leaves, animal fur and birds' feathers.

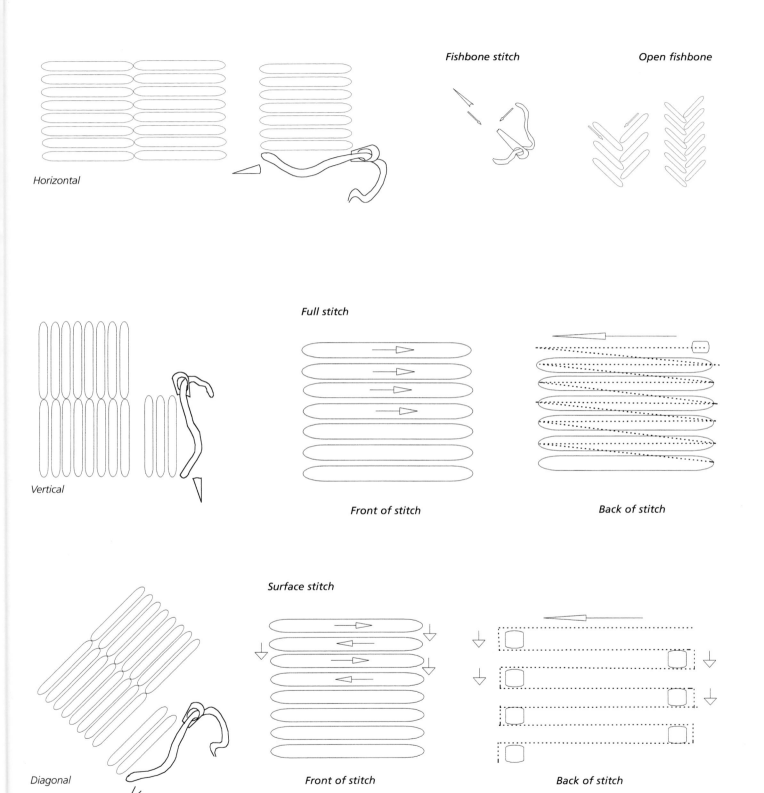

Fishbone stitch

Open fishbone

Horizontal

Full stitch

Vertical

Front of stitch

Back of stitch

Surface stitch

Diagonal

Front of stitch

Back of stitch

Design sheets

The 'design sheets' that appear in this chapter show designs taken from antique and modern pieces and are provided as a basis for practice and experiment. Templates are included, and colour selections from the Pearsall's Filoselle range are used to match as closely as possible the colours of the original piece. Where the colours on the original pieces are faded, the back of the embroidery has proved useful for colour matching.

The Filoselle thread was deemed to be the closest available alternative to genuine Chinese silk threads, as it has six strands that can be broken down into finer filaments to emulate the original Chinese versions (see

Above *Li shui border taken from a woman's dragon jacket, 19th century (also shown on the title page).*

page 48). For suppliers of genuine Chinese silk threads, see the Useful Addresses section at the end of the book.

Though the designs were originally stitched with Chinese silk threads in many shades and hues, for practical purposes a limited range of four to five hues is provided. Some designs offer an alternative set of colours, and some suggest the use of the new Pearsall's range of spaced dyed threads to fill in small motifs within a design.

The fineness or thickness of filaments used can determine the subtle change in colour, so a minimum of three to four hues can be used as a basic palette and six to eight hues to add more subtlety to a design. Extremely fine filaments, to increase contrast (using a darker shade) or reduce it (using a lighter shade), may be used as a finishing touch. Other effects can be achieved by blending a dark and a light shade together. For example, $^{1}/_{4}$ of a split strand in a dark shade can be blended with a finer filament (approximately $^{1}/_{8}$) of a lighter shade and vice versa.

If you are using spaced dyed threads, prepare them for stitching as follows. Undo the whole skein and decide where to cut each individual length. Thread length can vary from approximately 25–30cm (10–12in), to contain a mixture from light to dark or vice versa. Different effects can be achieved by manipulating the thread lengths and choosing which part of the cut filament to work with.

It is also possible to adapt the given colour scheme to other ranges of silk and non-silk threads such as Madeira stranded silk, Anchor and other stranded cotton, or de Havilland spaced dyed threads. The only point to remember is that the end product will be different.

The designs may also be adapted by choosing alternative methods of application. The original fabric used is provided for reference, but it can be replaced with medium-weight silk in a similar base colour to the original, or white or cream.

Design sheet 1 Li shui border

Most dragon robes and jackets have the bottom part embroidered with a very effective straight or wavy stripe design, the *li shui* border. Generally stitched on large areas, embroiderers usually preferred the surface stitch method, as it saved time and reduced the quantities of threads used. Different versions of the *li shui* border can be found on several museum examples of costumes from the Qing Dynasty. Designs can be worked in diagonal and vertical satin stitch using the surface or full stitch method. The thread colours may vary, as the design may either be stitched in four or five shades of one hue or in several shades of compatible colours. This border design, worked in shades of blue outlined in single gold thread, is from a woman's dragon jacket, which is shown more fully on the title page of this book.

Below *Li shui border stitch direction*

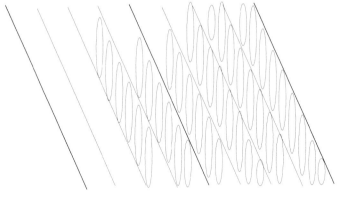

Base fabric Red silk satin.
Embroidery Diagonal satin stitch, couched threads.
Colours Porcelain Blue 293, 294; Delft Blue 25, 26, 29; Azuline Blue 56; gold threads.
Notes In this design the blue stripes are worked in a repeated set of four pairs of dark and light threads. Each pair of colours is separated by single couched gold threads.

The working sequence is as follows:

1st pair:	Column 1 Azuline Blue 56	Column 2	Porcelain Blue 294
2nd pair:	Column 3 Porcelain Blue 293	Column 4	Delft Blue 25
3rd pair:	Column 5 Delft Blue 29	Column 6	Delft Blue 26
4th pair:	Column 7 Porcelain Blue 294	Column 8	Porcelain Blue 293

Design sheet 2 Stylized blue bat

This design, embroidered here in shades of blue, is taken from a 19th-century man's robe and depicts a stylized bat. Bats are one of the most popularly used auspicious symbols of good luck and designs of this motif come in many shapes, sizes and forms, and on many different antique textiles. In this stylized design, the body of the bat has been merged with the wings of a butterfly, to create a motif that is sometimes known as a cicada.

Base fabric Navy blue silk satin.
Embroidery Satin stitch (horizontal, vertical and diagonal), split stitch for the antennae.
Colours This design is worked in white plus four shades of Delft Blue: dark 030; medium 029; pale 027; light 025.
Notes Voiding is left between areas of stitching. Supplementary stitches are sometimes added to connect areas or add details.

Alternative colours The colours in this design can be replaced, using any other set of plain colours, such as:
Cornflower blue: Dark 252; medium 251; pale 250; light 249.
Orange yellow: Dark 153; medium 152; pale 151; light 148.
Violet: Dark 262; Blue violet medium 044; pale 042; light 040.
or with spaced dyed thread from the Pearsall's Filoselle range, such as Cornish Blue, Tangerine Dream or Ultra Violet.

Satin stitch shading

During the course of my research into the general methods of work used within the satin stitch group of stitches, certain anomalies cropped up. In order to clarify this section, I have divided the stitches into three groups, highlighting the subtle variations that occur between the various methods of application. Though there are similarities between the stitches, there are also slight differences.

This range of stitches is generally used to imitate colour blending in paintings and also forms part of the basic stitches used for double-sided and double-faced embroidery. The stitches allow the embroiderer to depict flowers, leaves, fur and feathers with a lifelike subtlety and brilliance.

Satin stitch shading: Close knit stitches

The close knit stitches are broken down into three types: single layer shading, double layer shading and multiple layer shading.

Single layer shading

This technique uses long and short stitches alternately, placed side by side without overlapping. The technique is used to depict naturalistic designs featuring plants, flowers, furry animals, birds' wings and so on. This stitch is also referred to as 'single close knit stitch' or 'long and short stitch'.

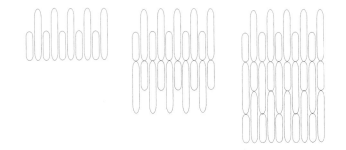

Single layer shading: long and short

Double layer shading

In this technique, comparatively long stitches are laid closer to each other in a staggered manner, to create a denser appearance than that produced by single layer shading. To enable easy blending, slightly shorter stitches are used where there is a colour change. The technique is often used to embroider minute details, such as the wings of butterflies, or the tails and feathers of birds. This stitch is also referred to as 'double close knit stitch'.

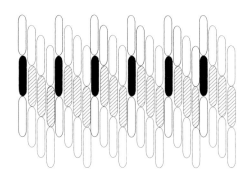

Double layer shading: long stitches in staggered lines

Multiple layer shading

There are several methods of application falling within this category. Stitches of equal or variable lengths are arranged in staggered lines following the shape of a design. The stitch direction runs from the outside edge of a design to the inner part. Stitches within this category are referred to as 'multiple close knit stitch'. The two most popular stitches are *shan tao* and *ping tao*.

Author's note

The word *layer* may appear to be misrepresented within this context as it refers to the threads 'laid down' in subsequent rows of stitching. Nevertheless, when fine threads are used, areas within a design are sometimes embroidered over and over again, thus building up layers of threads.

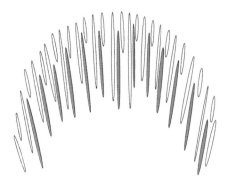

First row white

Multiple layer shading: *shan tao* stitch

This is the most popular and widely used method that falls within the multiple layer group. Stitches of varying length, applied with medium to finer threads, allow easy blending of colours. This method is used for double-sided embroidery and can be adapted for use in double-faced embroidery. The stitches are aligned towards the centre of the design so that when the centre is approached, the innermost stitches can be hidden. Within the Chinese stitch vocabulary, this stitch is also referred to as 'scattered stitch'.

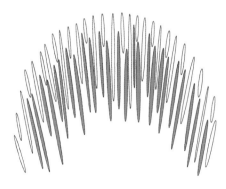

Second row red

First row: start with a long stitch and work alternate long and short stitches of variable lengths.

Second row: Make a long stitch between every second stitch of the last row, keeping to the same rough stitch length. Repeat this for subsequent rows.

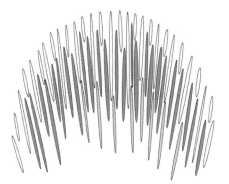

Third row blue

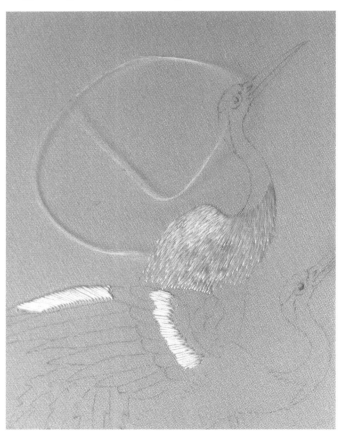

Fourth row yellow

Above Shan tao *stitch in progress, based on the painting given right.*

62

Multiple layer shading: *ping tao* stitch

This technique uses straight stitches that progress evenly within the shape of a design. When small motifs are embroidered using the *ping tao* method, colour blending is easily achieved, as each row can be worked starting from a light to dark shade (or vice versa) of the same colour of thread.

First row: Lay down stitches of the same length.

Second row: Place a stitch of the same length between each stitch of the previous row.

Third row: Lay down longer stitches, connected with the ends of the stitches of the first row.

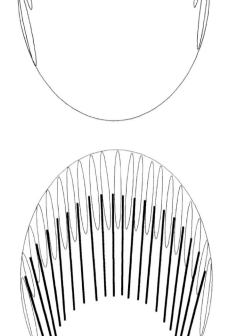

First row

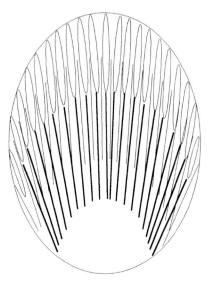

Second row: black lines

The stitches in the third row are linked to those of the first row.

Above *Part of a painted design, used as inspiration for stitch (left).*

63

Mixed straight stitch: *souhe* stitch

The *souhe* stitch technique uses alternate irregular long and short stitches, leaving visible spaces between stitches, and is also known as 'mixed straight stitch'. Colour gradation is easily achieved by blending tones and shades of the same colour to produce a natural and realistic effect. It is usually employed for portraying inert objects such as tree trunks, rocks and stones, but it can also be used to stitch flowers.

Stitches are worked from the inside top edge of the design to the lower part. Colour blending is achieved by either working from light to dark or dark to light, according to the design.

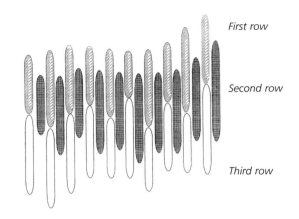
First row
Second row
Third row

The diagram on the top right shows how this stitch is achieved, following the steps below.

First row: Work vertical stitches of varying lengths from one end of the design to the other.

Second row: Work stitches of varying lengths between the spaces left by the first row.

Third row: Continue stitching from the bottom end of the stitches of the first row.

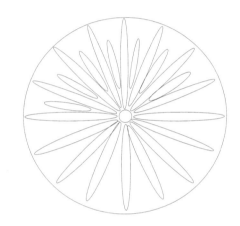
Vortex stitch

Vortex stitch: *shunxian* stitch

There is a variation of *souhe* stitch that is also known as '*shunxian* stitch' or 'vortex stitch'. In this technique, stitches are arranged in a radiating style, making it ideal for embroidering the rounded head and body shapes of animals. Long and short stitches are laid out alternately, starting from the centre and radiating outwards. Subsequent stitches are worked from the middle parting of the previously stitched row, again radiating outwards. This technique works well for any circular designs, such as the sun disc found on Mandarin badges of rank (see page 36) or general semi-circular shapes.

Above *Crane picture, 21st century. This modern design is worked in multiple layer (ping tao) stitch, with vortex stitch around the neck.*

Design sheet 3 Lotus flower and bud

The flowers, buds and leaves of this design (shown in full on page 116) have been embroidered using delicately shaded colours in *shan tao* stitch. Overlaid stitch (see page 62) has been applied to the vase and leaves.

Base fabric Cream medium-weight Habotai silk.
Embroidery Satin stitch, close knit stitches, stem stitch.
Colours Flowers, from light to dark in Golden Brown 001; Marigold 178, 180, 181, 183; Leaves in Grass Green 101, 104, 105, 107.
Notes Though the original picture has been stitched with fine filaments ranging approximately between one-eighth to one-twentieth, it is possible to work with a twentieth of Pearsall's Filoselle thread. The working method of this design is dictated by the individual elements of flower, buds and leaves – work can

progress from light to dark or vice versa. For the bud, use the medium colour, 181, to start the work at the tip of an individual petal, and use the darker colours last. The veins of the leaves are added on top of the embroidery using either stem stitch or a finer thread couched down. To increase or decrease the tonal values or to achieve a smooth grading from one colour to another, reduce the thread ply to a much finer filament than the one you have chosen to work with. This can be done either as the work progresses or when the embroidery is at an end.

Satin stitch shading: encroaching stitches

The different techniques within this category use a variety of long stitches, short stitches or combinations of both, applied according to the design. Within the Chinese embroidery vocabulary various names are given to each method of application. To simplify this group, I have selected the most popular techniques.

Block shading: *qiang* stitch

This technique uses short straight stitches, closely arranged row by row, according to the shape of the design. The stiches are linked in various ways, which may be altered to suit the design. The technique is used to depict flowers, birds and butterflies, especially their wings. Three-dimensional effects that are both realistic and decorative can be achieved by using subtle tones and shades of colour. Colour gradation is easily achieved. Voiding, which in the Chinese embroidery vocabulary is also known as 'water roads', may be left between the rows of stitching.

Qiang stitch can be further broken down into two categories: inward and outward *qiang*.

Inward *qiang*

When work starts from the outer top edge and follows the shape of the design to its inner part, this is referred to as inward *qiang*. The stitches of the second and subseque rows are aligned towards the centre of the design. T stitch is also referred to as *ping qiang* stitch.

First row: Use short, straight stitches to outline the ou edge of the design.

Second row: Work another row of short, straight stitch overlapping the end of the first row. This causes a ridge

Outward *qiang*

When the stitches are worked from the centre of t design to the outside edge, this is called outward qia Satin stitch is used for the first layer, then the stitches the second and subsequent rows are placed at the ends the stitches of the previous row, without overlapping. T stitches should progress in a neat and regular order, alw running in the same direction. This stitch is popula used to embroidery the wings of butterflies.

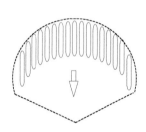

Inward qiang *stitch direction*   *Inward* qiang *method 1*

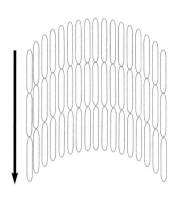

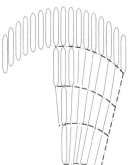

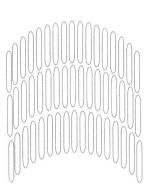

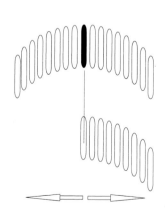

Qiang stitch   *Inward* qiang *method 2*   *Qiang stitch with voiding*   *Outward* qiang *stitch direction*

Design sheet 4 Spray of flowers on red

Design motifs featuring flowers and plants are very popular in Chinese embroidery, as each flower conveys a special meaning. This flower design, embroidered in subtle pink, blue, turquoise and green shades on a rich red background, recurs on several pieces of embroidered antique textiles dating from both the 19th and 20th centuries. The overall design has been embroidered using outward *qiang*, with the stem embroidered in satin stitch.

Base fabric Red medium-weight twill silk.
Embroidery Block shading (outward *qiang*) method and diagonal satin stitch.
Colours Four sets of colours from light to dark are given to work the flower petals and buds:
1st set in Wine Magenta Rose 173, 174, 175.
2nd set in Grape Purple 194, 195, 196.
3rd set in Pink 225, 226, 227.
4th set in Azuline Blue 50, 51, 52.
Leaves in Laurel Green 216, 218, 219.

Notes To stitch the flowers, start work with the lighter threads at the top of each petal, progressing to the darker thread for the inner part of the petal. Sometimes the reverse process is applied to the flower petals. To stitch the leaves, progress the shading from light on the outer tip to dark for the inner part. Combine colours 216 and 218 or 218 and 219 to add depth to the leaf.

Design sheet 5 Peaches

Designs showing peaches are very popular and can be found on several Chinese art and craft items, as this fruit is heavily endowed with symbolism. The wood of the peach tree was said to ward off demons and on New Year's Day it was a custom to place a bough from a peach tree at the gate of the house. The petals of the flowers were used in casting spells, and the fruit itself is regarded as a symbol of immortality.

Base fabric Red silk satin.
Embroidery Block shading (outward *qiang*) for the peaches and buds, leaves in inward *qiang*.
Colours Red peach in Scarlet 19, 20, 21, 22, 24; blue peach in Royal Blue 321, 322, 324, 325, 327; blue buds in Royal Blue 321, 322, 324; red buds in Scarlet 19, 20, 21; leaves in Green Blue 185, 187, 188; stem in Drab 47, 49.

Notes Peaches are worked from dark (outer edge) to pale (inner part), but for the buds and the leaves, colours are worked in reverse. The inner part is dark and the outer edge is light.
Alternative colours Spaced dyed thread can replace the plain colours: the red peach with Victoria Rose, the blue peach with either Crystal Waters or Cornish Blue, and Aegean Sea or St Andrews for the leaves.

Design sheet 6 Butterfly on red

In Chinese symbolism, the butterfly was often regarded as a lover, sipping nectar from the calyx of a flower, a female symbol. When plum blossom and the butterfly appear together, they represent long life and beauty.

Butterfly wing segments: Inward qiang method

First row: Bring the needle up in the centre at A.

Using vertical satin stitch, work from right to left. To work the other half, bring the needle back up at A and stitch from left to right.

Second row: Using two lengths of thread in the needle, bring the needle up through the fabric at B and hold in place with two tiny stitches. Stitching starts from the centre point, working from right to left.

Third row: Bring the needle back to the centre point C. Repeat the above.

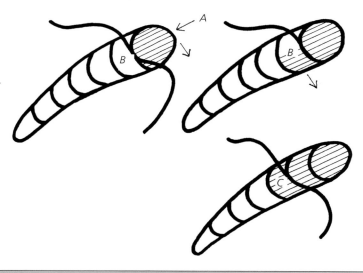

Base fabric Red medium-weight twill silk.

Embroidery Block shading (inward *qiang*), satin stitch, back stitch.

Colours Wing segments in White 88; outer edge in Delft Blue 30; between segments in Dull Peacock 117; overlaid stitch in Madder Pink 232A; back stitch in White 88; antenna in Delft Blue 30 and White 88 softly twisted together or spaced dyed Cornish Blue.

Notes This design is worked with finer thread filaments. Follow the diagrams to work the individual segments. Added touches include lines of back stitches in White 88 worked over every two threads of blue satin stitch. Also four tiny stitches in Madder Pink 232A are used to catch the centre and adjoining thread of each top segment to create a pattern. A supplementary stitch linking one part of the butterfly to another, also worked in Madder Pink 232A, is also used.

Design sheet 7 Butterfly on lilac

This beautifully embroidered design is taken from the edge of a woman's garment and is stitched in subtle shades of olive green, with contrasting colours of purple and blue, on a lovely lilac silk background fabric. In Chinese embroidery, designs depicting butterflies are often placed among flowers, and are sometimes coupled with the oriole bird and the willow tree, which are both regarded as symbols of femaleness.

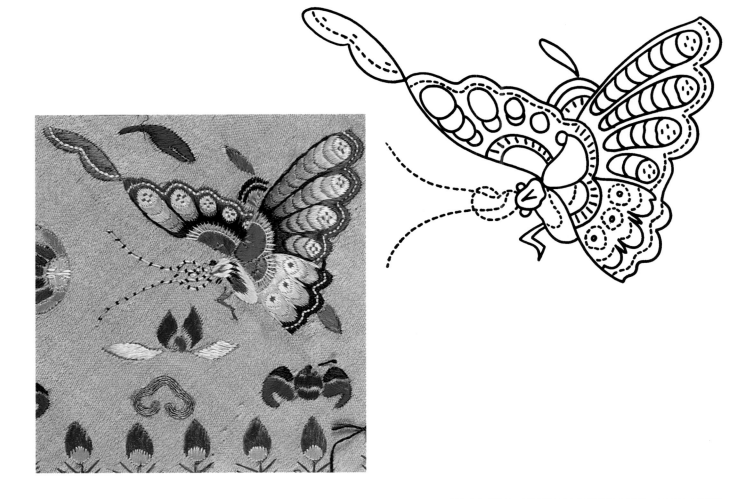

Base fabric Lilac silk satin.
Embroidery Block shading (inward *qiang*), satin stitch, back stitch
Colours Colours are given in order from the top to the bottom of each segment.
9 rows in Olive Green 245; Drab Green 348; Olive Green 246, 247, 248; Sage Green 191 x 2, 193 x 2. 7 rows in Olive Green 245; Drab Green 348; Olive Green 246, 247, 248; Sage Green 191, 193. 5 rows in Olive Green 245, 246, 247, 248; Sage Green 191. 3 rows in Olive Green 245, 246, 248. 2 rows in Olive Green 245, 246. Body of butterfly in Olive Green 245, 248; outer edge in Delft Blue 31; between segments in Olive Brown 138; satin stitch in Grape Purple 198; back stitch and antenna in Olive Green 245 couched with Olive Brown 138. 3 rows of blue segments in Steel Blue 72, 74, 75; outer edge 77; between segments in Nut Brown 240.

Scale carving stitch

Also referred to as fur simulation, this technique combines the *souhe* and *qiang* methods of work to produce a fan shape. It is used to depict the scales of dragons and fish, tigers' stripes, and the wings of insects and birds. This is a versatile stitch that is, with each application, dependent on the design. The methods of work are broken down into three types: scale piling, scale laying and scale binding.

Scale piling

Here, long and short stitches are set closely together to form scales. Each scale is worked individually in two steps and stitching starts from the centre of each scale and works out towards the edge. The scales thus formed are dense inside with a lighter, thinner edge.

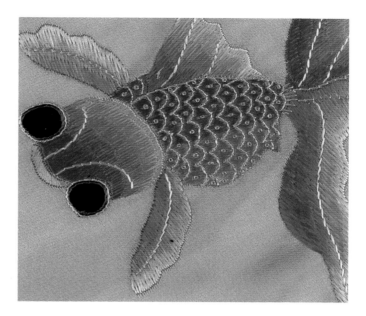

Above *Fish from a 20th-century panel, illustrating the use of scale carving. The centre of each scale has also been decorated with a single Pekin knot seed stitch.*

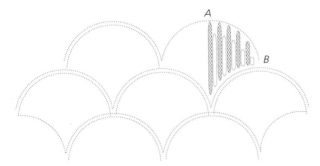

First row: step 1

First mark the area where the scale stitches are to be laid. Starting at the centre of the scale (A) with a full-length stitch, work out to the right towards B, alternating long and short stitches.

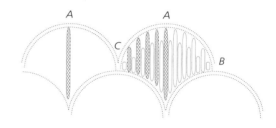

First row: step 2

Bring the needle back next to the left of the first centre stitch (A). Start with a short stitch and progress towards the left to C, alternating long and short stitches. Bring the needle to the centre of the next scale at A.

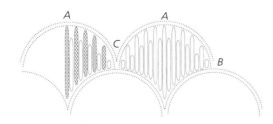

First row: step 3

Next and subsequent scales: work starts from the centre with a long stitch and progresses as in steps 1 and 2. Voiding is left between each scale.

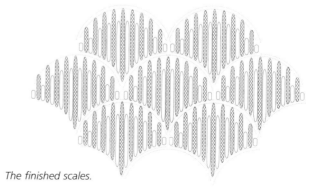

The finished scales.

71

Scale laying

Also known as *qianglin*, this technique uses satin stitches. The stitches are arranged neatly without overlapping, with each stitch decreasing in length to accommodate the form of the scale. The scales are worked individually in two steps. The right side of the scale is worked first and the stitch lengths are then mirror-imaged for the left side.

Note: With both scale piling and scale laying techniques, a back stitch can be added to give solidity. Alternatively, single gold threads or thick threads are sometimes used to create an outline in place of the voiding.

Above *Scale detail from mandarin duck, shown in full on page 9.*

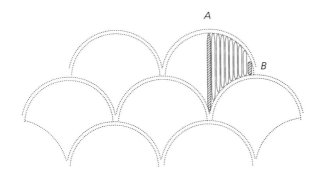

First row: step 1

First mark the area where the scale stitches are to be laid. Starting with a full-length stitch at the centre of the scale (A), work out to the right towards B, decreasing the length of each subsequent stitch.

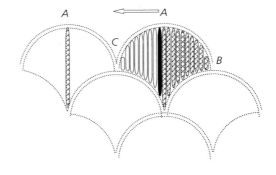

First row: step 2

Bring the needle back out to the left of the first stitch and work out to the left towards C, ensuring that the stitch lengths are a mirror image of the ones on the right-hand half of the scale. Finish by bringing the needle to the next scale at A and repeat steps 1 and 2.

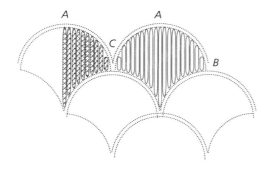

First row: step 3

Continue in the same way. As when scale piling, voiding is left between each scale.

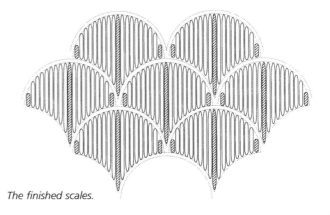

The finished scales.

Scale binding

Satin stitches are first laid down in one direction within the design area to form a foundation. These foundation stitches, which can be worked using either the full or surface satin stitch method, follow the direction of the scales (in other words, they lie over the scaly area, all going in the same direction). After this, backstitching is added on top, running in the opposite direction, to form the scale pattern by holding the foundation stitches down. Fairly long stitches can be used for the foundation, as the subsequent overstitching will hold them down. This technique can also be used to cover large areas and is not dissimilar to the technique of overlaid stitches.

Some preparation is required prior to starting this method of work. First, the design area has to be marked out and the correct scale size transferred to tracing paper and then to tissue or stitch-and-tear paper. Use the scales shown on the right as a guide.

As an alternative to back stitch, couching – perhaps with single or double gold threads – can be used to create the same effect.

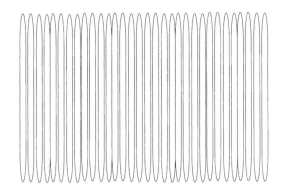

Step 1

Starting at the top left-hand corner of the area, lay a foundation row of satin stitches within the shape of the design.

Step 2

Place the tracing on top of the laid foundation. Starting from the bottom right-hand side of the design, work back stitches, following the direction of the scales.

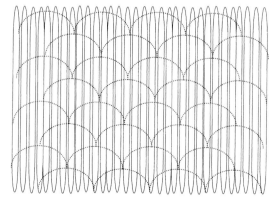

The finished scales.

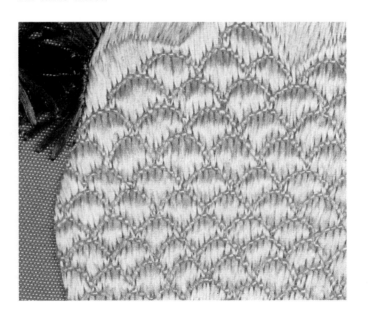

Above *Scale detail from Manchurian cranes picture, shown in full on page 119.*

73

Design sheet 8 – Red and yellow fish

Fish, one of the Buddhist symbols representing abundance, can also carry sexual connotations. As such, the love life of a happily married couple was sometimes described as 'the pleasures of fish in water'. A pair of fishes was a popular gift for a wedding, as it represented harmony and pleasure. The scales of the bright red and yellow fish in this twentieth-century embroidered picture are worked in scale carving stitches.

Base fabric Blue nylon.

Embroidery Close knit stitches (*shan tao*), overlaid stitches.

Colours Left-hand fish in Orange Yellow 149, 150, 152, 153 and Grass Green 103, 105; right-hand fish in Marigold 178, 179, 180, 181.

Notes This design may be worked in scale piling, laying or binding. If you are using the scale binding method, lay the foundation rows of satin stitch and work the overlaid scales parallel to the dotted centre line, as shown in the stitch direction diagram to the right. If you are using long and short stitches, angle them to follow the curve of the design. Though the design has been stitched using the *shan tao* method, it is possible to use long floating satin stitches as a base before working the scales.

Alternative colours The base colours can be replaced with spaced dyed threads as follows: Yellow fish in Harvest Gold; orange fish in Tangerine Dream; pine needle leaves and water bubble in St Andrews.

Overlaid stitch

This very versatile stitch is formed with a foundation layer of plain satin stitch or one of its variations, after which patterns in geometric or circular format are stitched on top, in the same way as in the scale-binding method. Embellishments such as couched gold threads, sequins, beads or buttons can also be added. When long and short stitches are used as the foundation layer, the stitches create a compact and solid base upon which couching is easily worked.

Method of work

Prior to stitching the foundation layer, choose and prepare the pattern to be overlaid. For accurate stitching of the patterns, set squares or a piece of card may be used to create guidelines. Alternatively, individual patterns can be transferred either to tracing or stitch-and-tear paper, then placed and held down over the area of design with a few anchor stitches.

Above *Embroidered ladies on a sleeveband, 19th century. Examples of patterns using overlaid stitches on the bottoms of the ladies' skirts.*

Step 1

The foundation layer may be worked in a range of satin stitches, including horizontal, vertical or diagonal stitches, filling the design area with regular long stitches. Alternatively, long and short stitches may be used, as shown here.

Step 2

Secure the tracing paper pattern over the stitched foundation area with a few holding stitches and stitch the overlaid pattern through the layers of paper, stitch and fabric, removing the paper carefully when stitching is done.

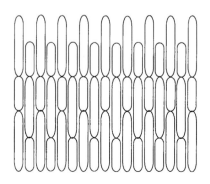

Long and short stitch foundation layer

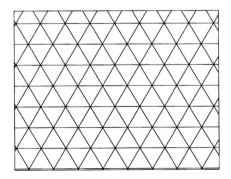

Pattern to be overlaid

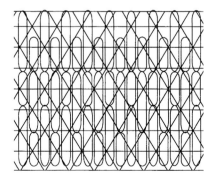

Overlaid pattern over foundation layer

Overlaid stitch patterns (diaper patterns)

Lattice and other types of repeated patterns are popularly used in Chinese designs. They are endlessly adapted, either to feature as border patterns on decorative objects or applied to textiles, as seen on the bottom of the woman's skirt on page 75 or on the lattice design on the pair of sleevebands on page 17. The patterns shown here, which have been taken from several sources, can be adapted for use with the overlaid stitch technique. Essentially, any design that forms a repeating grid-like pattern can be used. Antique beads and sequins, small buttons and pearls, as well as a variety of metal threads, may be applied to create a rich texture.

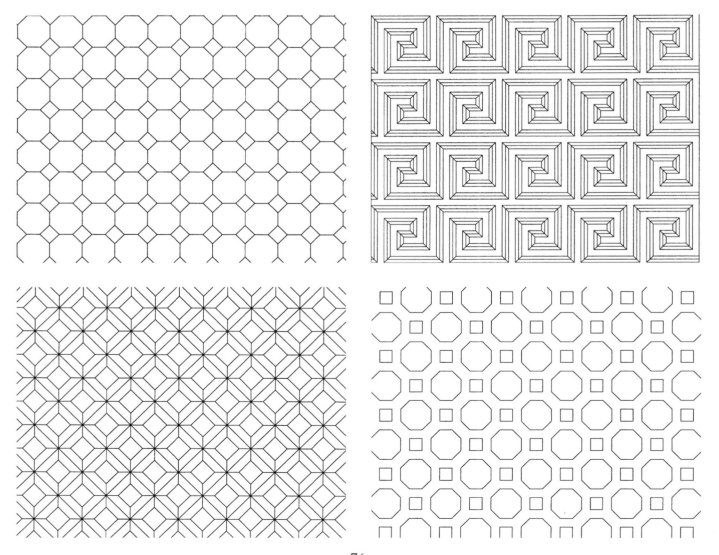

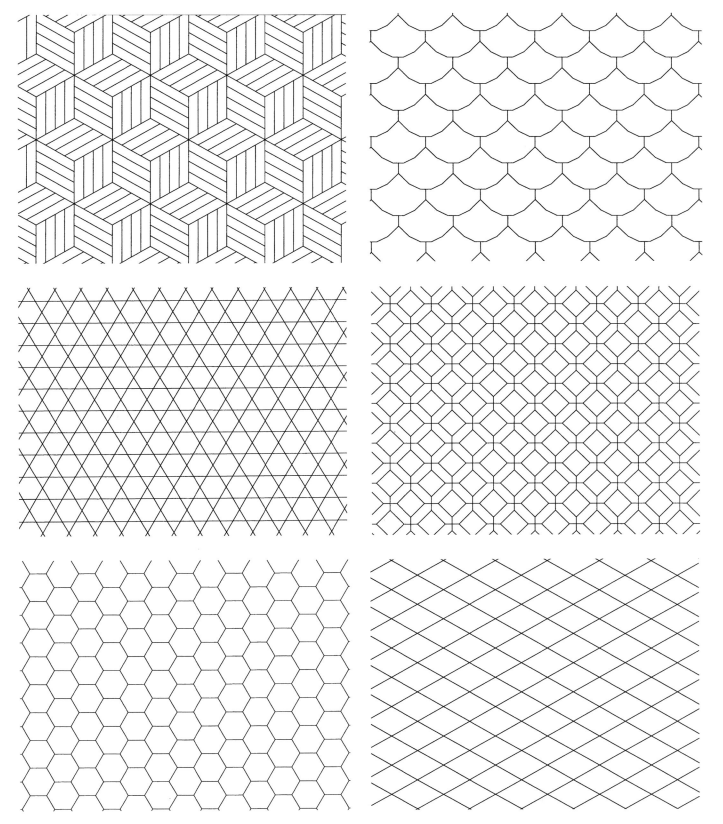

Design sheet 9 Blue vase

Vases carried a symbolic meaning of peace, but could also have a number of further symbolic meanings depending on the different varieties of flowers and plants that were depicted with them. This modern embroidered picture of a vase uses complex overlaid stitches, worked over a satin stitch foundation, to pleasing effect.

Base fabric White nylon.
Embroidery Overlaid stich and satin stitch.
Notes The blue vase picture is as an example of overlaid stitches using reversible techniques worked in a mixture of close knit stitches and vertical satin stitch. The intricate overlaid design has been worked with a finer thread than the base. Use the small jar template as a guide to try out several methods of application, overlaying diaper patterns as set out on pages 76–77.

Raised embroidery

For this technique, the ground fabric has to be prepared by being raised, either with card or other materials, such as thread, tissue paper, pelmet Vilene or wadding (polyester or silk). The embroidery is worked after the area has been prepared. This technique is useful for creating realistic effects when depicting animals' eyes or similar small areas of a design. Any of the following methods can be used to achieve this effect.

Method 1

Threads thicker than those to be used for the embroidery are laid within the design area and couched down, either horizontally or vertically, in the opposite direction to that of the embroidery.

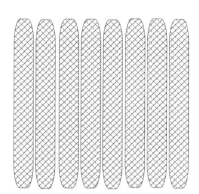

*Step 1: lay a vertical foundation layer
of satin stitch in thick threads.*

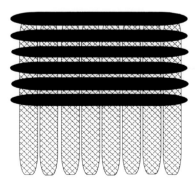

*Step 2: Stitch over the foundation
layer with horizontal satin stitches.*

Method 2

For this method, soft card, pelmet Vilene or layers of acid-free tissue paper are cut slightly smaller than the required design and held in place, either with stitches or PVA glue. If glue is used, the fabric must be allowed to dry before stitching. Using a template of the raised design area, cut pieces smaller than the design, leaving approximately 12mm (1/2in) all around. For a more subtle, rounded effect, subsequent layers can be cut slightly smaller than the previous layer, as shown. This method provides a sharp edge and gives the embroidery a slightly stiff look.

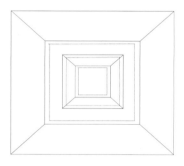

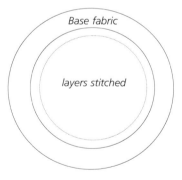

Base fabric

layers stitched

Method 3

For a softer appearance, various thickness of wadding may be used. Cut out a stencil in card and place this over the wadding to mark the shape before cutting it out. Hold the wadding in place with stitches and then embroider the raised surface. The Chinese method is to use layers of paper instead of wadding.

Knot stitches

Another group of stitches popularly used in traditional Chinese embroidery are the knot stitches. Referred to as the *tuan chen*, the most important stitch in this group, in so far as it is the most commonly used, is the Pekin knot, but other variations, such as the long-tailed knot, are also used.

Pekin knot

This stitch is known under several names, including Chinese knot, seed stitch, blind stitch, forbidden stitch and point de Pekin. The technique produces a knot that can be applied in various ways: as an outline, to fill a design, to depict the stamens of flowers or in combination with other stitches. The general method of work is to twist the thread *once* or *twice* around the needle to produce a knot. It is important to note a few points when using this stitch.

- It may be worked clockwise or anticlockwise, to accommodate the design.
- The fineness, thickness, quality and type of thread that is used determine the quality and look of the finished embroidery.
- Second and subsequent rows of knots are laid between the stitches of the previous row to form a neat and solid stitched area, with no gaps.
- The direction at which the needle enters the fabric determines the angle of the stitch. It is therefore important to maintain the same stitching direction in order to produce a neat and uniform finish.

The Pekin knot falls into two categories – seed stitch and solid stitch. If, as the knot is formed, the thread is twisted *once* around the needle, the stitch is referred to as seed stitch. The resulting knot is hollow, in that it has a hole in the middle, and resembles a slanted capital Q. Fine-to-medium threads work well with this technique. If the thread is twisted *twice* around the needle, then the stitch is referred to as a solid knot because it produces a heavier and more compact effect. The use of medium-to-thicker threads for this technique gives a denser quality to the work.

The Pekin knot has been referred to as 'blind stitch' and 'forbidden stitch', but there is no evidence to substantiate the notion that embroiderers went blind over-using this stitch and as a result were forbidden to use it. The name forbidden stitch might also refer to the stitch being used extensively by embroiderers who came from the Forbidden City. These explanations are presumed to have been passed orally from generation to generation.

Left *Couple in a garden from skirt panel, 19th century. The couple are embroidered in overlaid encroaching stitches; the rest of the panel uses Pekin knot stitch. Each element is outlined with a single gold thread.*

Author's note

I have found that the Pekin knot and the French knot are one and the same stitch. This is based on my extensive use of French knots since childhood and my subsequent experiments with Chinese knots since starting this research. To help clarify confusion over this stitch I have asked some embroiderers and teachers of embroidery that I have been involved with, both here and in China, to demonstrate and provide samples of their French or Pekin knots. The resulting samples showed that the stitches were identical.

A possible explanation for this confusion and the different names may lie in a comment made by Abbé de Montault that nuns, who had learned the stitch from girls in an orphanage, may have brought the stitch from China and transferred it to the French repertoire of stitches. In earlier days, the French knot was produced with one twist round the needle. This has changed over the years and nowadays it is produced with two twists. This development, and the variations in the working methods of right- or left-handed embroiderers, combined with their different approaches to its application, either clockwise or anticlockwise (see step 2, overleaf) may have led to the differences in the printed diagrams produced by subsequent authors to demonstrate the technique. In conclusion, though the working diagrams in this book are based on my method of producing this stitch, and may not be dissimilar to working diagrams found in other texts on the subject, individual embroiderers should use the method with which they feel most comfortable, as long as the resulting stitch is the same.

General notes

Before starting the Pekin knot it is useful to note the following: for a neat, uniform finish, always insert the needle into the fabric at the same angle. If the working method is the reverse of that shown below – in other words, the needle is placed *over* the thread, which is then twisted in the opposite direction – the slant of the stitches thus formed will be reversed.

Though step 2 of the Pekin knot (seed and solid) is illustrated with the thread taken in a clockwise direction, the stitches can also be worked anticlockwise.

For both seed and solid stitches, first anchor the thread with an invisible dot and bring the needle out on top of the fabric at the starting position, A.

Above *Detail from a sleeveband depicting animals and symbols, embroidered in Pekin knot seed stitch and outlined with a heavily twisted thread. Courtesy of Meg Andrews.*

Seed stitch

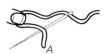

Step 1 *Bring the needle out at A and place it under the thread. Hold the thread with the left hand.*

Step 2 *Twist the thread once around the needle.*

Step 3 *Pull the thread tight around the needle.*

Step 4 *Insert the needle back into the fabric at B.*

Step 5 *Tighten thread and push the needle through the fabric.*

   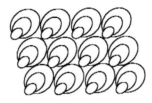

Step 6 *Pull firmly. A seed stitch is formed.*

Step 7 *Bring the needle back on top to start the next stitch.*

Step 8 *Continue to produce a single row of seed stitches.*

Step 9 *Subsequent rows of stitches are placed between those of the previous rows.*

Solid stitch

Step 1 *Bring the needle out at A and place it under the thread. Hold the thread with the left hand.*

Step 2 *Twist the thread twice around the needle.*

Step 3 *Pull the thread tight around the needle.*

Step 4 *Insert the needle back into the fabric at B.*

Step 5 *Tighten thread and push the needle through the fabric.*

Step 6 *Pull firmly. A solid stitch is formed.*

Step 7 *Bring the needle back on top to start the next stitch.*

Step 8 *Continue to produce a solid row of seed stitches.*

Step 9 *Subsequent rows of stitches are placed between those of the previous rows.*

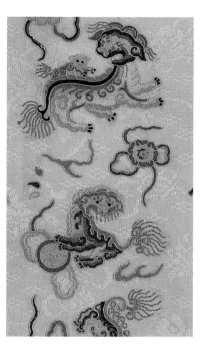

Right *Sleeveband, early 19th century. Showing the 'Dogs of Fo', this design is a very fine and exquisitely embroidered example of Pekin knot seed stitch and couched gold threads. This kind of barely visible stitch may have given rise to the 'forbidden stitch' legend and a magnifying glass must be used to appreciate the workmanship. The light gauze base fabric consists of a pattern weave of various auspicious symbols.*

Long-tailed knot

Often used to depict flowers, the long-tailed knot can be formed using the seed or solid stitch method. It is a popular stitch used in folk embroidery to create a patterned background. Follow steps 1–3 of seed or solid stitch. To make the tail of the knot, reinsert the needle 1cm ($^1/_2$in) away from the first exit.

A long-tailed knot is formed with Pekin knot solid stitch.

The next stitch starts at C.

Single row of long-tailed knots.

Double row of long-tailed knots.

Long-tailed knots used for flowers.

Above *Two men in a boat, from a late 19th-century sleeveband. This design has been finely embroidered with tiny seed stitches that are barely visible to the naked eye.*

Design sheet 10 Blue peony

This design was originally worked in seed stitch, but solid stitch may be used if preferred. There are four blue shades in the peony, ranging from pale to dark. Those in the petals are stitched from dark to light.

Use one or two strands of thread in the needle to stitch this design, and follow stitch instructions for your chosen stitch. When Pekin knots are used as a filling stitch for a flower, the stitches may be worked from right to left, following the outline of the design. Petals are assessed and worked individually. Always start by securing the thread with a couple of invisible dots.

Start by tracing and transferring the basic design to fabric, from the picture below. Broken lines (diagram A) indicate the first rows of the petals, which are worked in the darkest colour. Petals marked X are stitched in this colour only. The numbers and rows (diagrams B and C) indicate the number of rows per petal. The leaves are embroidered with satin stitches.

C

A

B

Base fabric Orange-red silk.
Embroidery Pekin knot seed stitch.
Colours Steel Blue 76, 75, 74, 72.
Notes Follow the diagrams. One strand of Pearsall's Filoselle can be used without removing the twist. Alternatively, solid stitch can be used to fill the design area.
Alternative colours The blue colours can be replaced with a different set of colours, for example, Pomegranate 281, 280, 279, 277; Rose 85, 81, 80, 78; or spaced dyed Victorian Rose.

Pekinese stitch

Described as a 'back stitch with a loop', this stitch is worked by starting with a foundation row of back stitches through which loops are then formed. The technique is traditionally referred to as silk locking or pulling stitch.

There are two methods of working: the first, or one-needle method, is to create the stitch effect by stitching the foundation row first and then weaving the thread in between the stitches; the second method, or two-needle technique, is to thread two needles and work the foundation and looping simultaneously.

Both methods of work are time-consuming, and patience is required to master the two-needle technique. However, although I personally favour the one-needle technique, it is well worth making the effort to try the two-needle technique, as the stitch produced is even and neat in appearance. The two-needle technique also has the advantage of circumventing the problems that may be encountered with the one-needle method (see below).

Threads

Though any type of threads can be used, commercially twisted threads such as Mulberry silk, Gütermann silk or coton perlé work well with this stitch.

An experimental approach

As two threads are used for this stitch, a new dimension can be added by using two different colours or type of threads. For example the back stitches can be worked in one colour and the loops in a contrasting colour. For a contemporary approach, thicker threads or metal threads may be used for the loops.

Success with the one-needle method

With the one-needle technique, care must be taken to keep a neat appearance. The problems that I have encountered using the one-needle technique relate mostly to the type of thread used. For example, when floss silk is used, the needle tends to catch the backstitch thread of the foundation row and this disturbs the neatness of the stitch. This problem is recurrent, especially when subsequent rows are stitched to fill a design. To minimize the damage, it is advisable to use tapestry needles to form the loops, after the foundation row has been stitched.

Another problem that can arise with the one-needle technique occurs when it is used as a filling stitch, as uneven gaps may appear between each row of stitching. This happens because, to achieve even spacing, the starting point of the second row should relate to the height of stitches from the first row. The problem is easily resolved by stitching a couple of sample rows, using the

Left *Scene from a sleeveband, 19th century or earlier. This is a rare example of Pekinese stitch that has been used to outline and part-fill a design area.*

intended embroidery thread, in order to gauge the distance for the next foundation row of back stitches. This process has to be repeated every time a different thickness of thread is used.

Back stitch foundation.

One-needle method

Step 1

Start by making a foundation row of back stitches. The stitching can begin at either the right or left of the fabric.

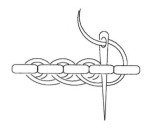

Pekinese stitch with loops worked above the back stitch row.

Step 2

Bring the needle to the top of fabric and pass it through the back stitches of the foundation row, following the diagrams above right, to form the loops. The loops can be worked either above or below the foundation line, depending on the design.

A single row of Pekinese stitch can be used to outline a design, while multiple rows form a useful filling stitch.

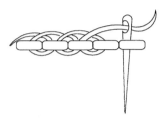

Pekinese stitch with loops worked below the back stitch row.

Single row of Pekinese stitch with loops formed above.

Two-needle method

In the two-needle method, two threads are used simultaneously to work the whole stitch. Thread two needles, one for the foundation row of back stitches and one for the loops (these may be worked in the same or contrasting threads). The first needle makes the back stitches and the second makes the loops.

Three rows of finished Pekinese stitch, as used to fill an area.

Double Pekinese stitch

Another variation of Pekinese stitch, this stitch is also known as double pulling stitch or herringbone ladder filling stitch. Firstly, two rows of backstitching are placed a distance apart from each other. Then a second thread is used to link the parallel threads, using a figure-of-eight action. The loops are formed above the top and bottom of the parallel back stitches. The backstitching can be varied by being close-set or spaced apart. This stitch can be very effective when used decoratively.

Left *Another scene taken from the sleeveband shown on page 86.*

Design sheet 11 Pavilion and scenery

Multi-cornered pavilions in a variety of shapes and sizes are recurrent designs popularly found on sleevebands. The pavilions themselves are regarded as sources of shelter for travellers or may be the scene for a romantic meeting between two people. This pavilion, taken from a sleeveband, is surrounded by trees and water.

Base fabric Cream silk.

Embroidery Pekinese stitch in single and multiple rows.

Colours Cloud above pavilion in China Blue 209, Golden Brown 006A; willow tree trunk in Golden Brown 006A, leaves in Sage Green 190; tree behind pavilion: trunk in Golden Brown 006A; leaves in Sage Green 191 and Olive Green 246. Pavilion windows in Azuline Blue 056, China Blue 206, 209; pavilion roof in Brown 317, 319; top of roof in China Blue 206, 209, Golden Brown 006.

Notes As the colours on the front of the sleeveband from which this design was taken have faded with time, the selected colours offered are a combination of the original colours taken from the back of the embroidery, and the muted colours of the front.

Design sheet 12 Vases

When Pekinese stitch is used to fill an area, consideration should be given as to whether the loops are to be formed above or below the foundation line and whether stitching is to start from the inner part of the design and work towards the outer edge, or begin from the outer part and work inwards. It is advisable to make a sample embroidery first, in order to gauge the height of the loops and thus determine the ideal spacing between rows and calculate the number of rows of back stitching that will be required to fill the design area.

For circular designs, the two-needle method works best and stitching can be worked either from the centre to the edge or vice versa. Loops can also be formed either below or above the back stitches.

Base fabric Cream silk.
Embroidery Pekinese stitch in multiple rows to fill the design.
Colours Bottom of vase in Delft Blue 25, 26, 28, 29, 30; Azuline Blue 057; Olive Brown 137, 138; Olive Green 248; Willow Green 256a.

Notes As with Design Sheet 11, the colours on the front of the sleeveband from which this design was taken have faded with time, so the selected colours offered are a combination of the original colours taken from the back of the embroidery and the muted colours of the front.

Above *A selection of 18th- and 19th-century accessories: fan case, mirror holder, and purses embroidered and appliquéd with auspicious motifs.*

Other stitches

Split stitch

This stitch offers a quick and easy way of filling large areas of a design. It is also used as an outline, especially when flowers are embroidered with satin stitch. Below is an example of split stitch used to embroider a *li shui* border.

Split stitch

Above *Detail from dragon robe showing the use of split stitch.*

Back stitch

This produces a neat line and is used on its own to embroider curved and long lines, such as hair or fish fins, or in other decorative combinations, as in Pekinese stitch.

Back stitch

Laced back stitch

This stitch, also known as binding stitch, is similar to stem stitch, except that it is more solid and durable. Laced back stitch is popular in northern China and is used to embroider pillow slips and curtains for doors.

It is a very simple stitch: back stitching is laid as a foundation, and this is then laced with another thread of the same colour or a different shade.

Stem stitch

The Chinese name for this stitch is gun stitch and its application is slightly different to the Western approach as it is more precise. Also referred to as rolling stitch, rod-like, pulling or willow stitch, this quick and easy stitch is used, as the name suggests, to embroider the stems of plants, flowers, branches or any part of a design that requires a linear effect. It produces a fine twisted line that can also be used to edge patterns or accentuate a design line.

Stem stitch is also useful as a filling stitch. It works well when used to stitch a tree trunk, for example, as it creates a solid, textured effect, similar to that of split stitch. This stitch sometimes replaces the split or back stitch used to edge a design before it is embroidered.

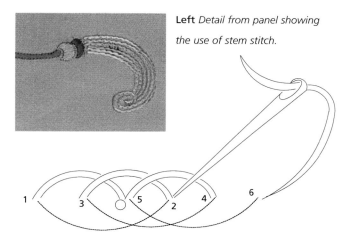

Left *Detail from panel showing the use of stem stitch.*

Stem stitch working direction

Running stitch

Also called pushing stitch, this is used to fill empty spaces and should be evenly spaced out at regular intervals.

Chain stitch and its variations

Chain stitch is another highly versatile stitch, with many variations that are popular in Chinese embroidery.

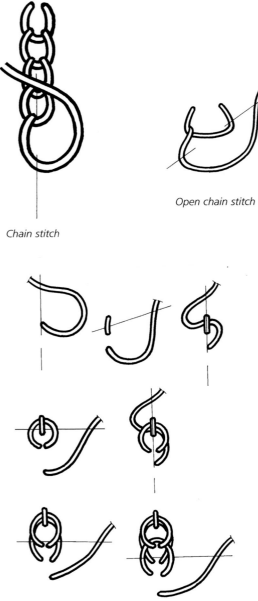

Chain stitch

Open chain stitch

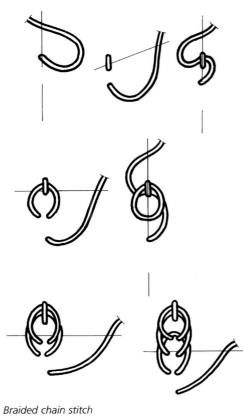

Braided chain stitch

Heavy chain stitch

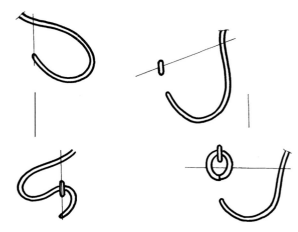

Broad chain stich

Other useful stitches

Fly stitch, which can be worked singly or in vertical rows, for a stem-like effect, is also much used. Other popular stitches with an open appearance include feather stitch, fern stitch and pine needle stitch.

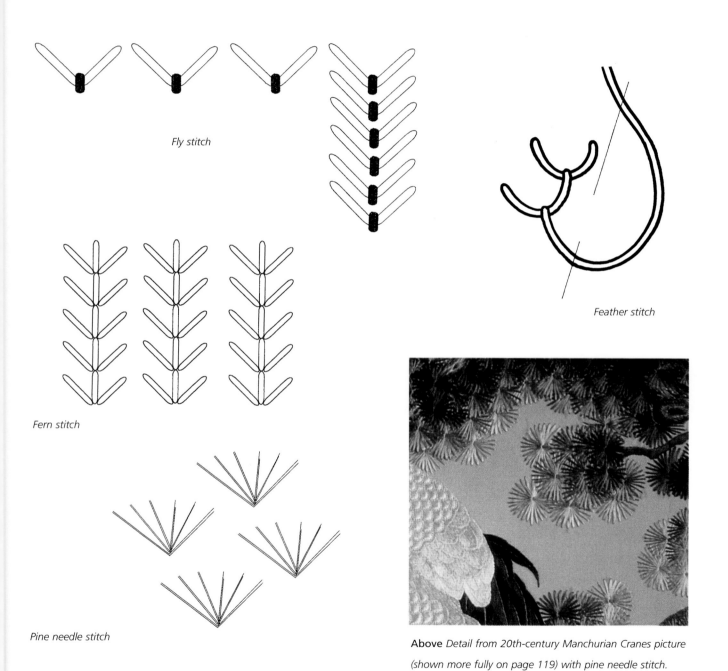

Fly stitch

Feather stitch

Fern stitch

Pine needle stitch

Above *Detail from 20th-century Manchurian Cranes picture (shown more fully on page 119) with pine needle stitch.*

93

Design sheet 13 Dragon head with peacock feathers

This design is taken from a late 19th-century woman's jacket (pictured in full on the title page). Filaments taken from peacock feathers are couched to create the dragon's flowing mane. Peacock feathers were used extensively during the Qing Dynasty as decorative elements on hats and other accessories, often twisted with silk or metallic threads. The number of filaments used together depends on the thickness required for the design.

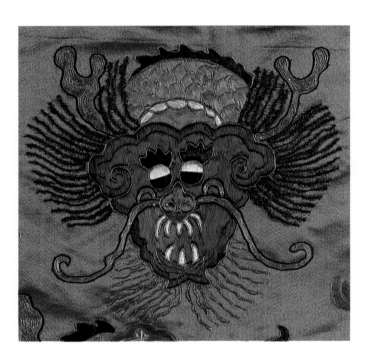

Peacock feathers

Base fabric Red silk.
Embroidery Satin stitch variations, couched threads and feathers, with raised embroidery for the eyes.
Colours Face centre in Porcelain Blue 294; face edge in Azuline Blue 056; top of head in Porcelain Blue 293; eyes in Azuline Blue 057; nose in Mocha 306; eyes and teeth in Snow White 314; mouth in Rose 084; Gold threads and peacock feathers (Imitation Jap gold T70 may be used for outlines).

Notes This design is taken from the woman's dragon jacket (also featured on the title page) and shows the peacock feathers used to highlight the whiskers. See opposite page for instructions on how to couch peacock feathers. Fine machine embroidery gold mix threads can be used for couching.

Step 1 Take the number of filaments required (between two and four) from a feather and fold them in half.

A

Step 2 Secure the fold at the centre (A) with a back stitch

Step 3 Working on the right side, twist the filaments gently in an S or Z twist and couch them down, either using threads of a matching colour or fine gold thread.

Step 4 Finish the other side of the fold in the same way. Repeat as shown to simulate the dragon's whiskers.

Couching Metal threads

There are several ways of couching metal threads on to embroidery, either to fill an area or as an edging stitch. Here are a few of the key techniques.

Two ways of beginning couching

How to turn the thread round at the end of a row

Two ways of finishing off the couched thread

Part of an early 19th-century dragon robe, depicting a five-clawed dragon, displaying the use of couched gold threads.

Design sheet 14 Cat

In some parts of China, the cat is regarded as a bad omen, but in others it represents good luck. The word for 'cat', *mao*, is phonetically close to that for 'octegenarian', so it can also symbolize longevity. If a cat is depicted with butterflies or plum and bamboo, it implies the wish of long life for the recipient of the embroidery.

Base fabric Green nylon.
Embroidery Close knit stitch (*shan tao*), satin stitch, stem stitch.
Colours Face in Snow White 314; nose in Orange Yellow 155; ribbon in Military Red 304; ears in Madder Pink 232.
Right eye Inner circle of horizontal satin stitch in Brown 317; vertical satin stitch in Black 89; first circular outline in stem stitch using White 314; second outline in Olive Brown 134; outside edge: Brown 319. **Left eye** Inner circle of horizontal satin stitch in Azuline Blue 056; vertical satin stitch in Black 89; first circular

outline in stem stitch using White 314; second outline in Azuline Blue 053; outside edge in Brown 319.
Notes To work this design, start by embroidering the ears and the ribbon. Progress with the centre of the eye, leaving the outer edge. Start to embroider the cat's face before finishing the outer edge of the eyes, followed by the nose and whiskers. It is possible to achieve a double-sided effect if great care is taken as work progresses and directional stitches are applied following the shape of the design.

Design sheet 15 Trees

These embroidered trees have been taken from the waistcoat opposite and show how the choice of stitch technique makes all the difference when depicting the individual characteristics of a particular type of tree.

Base fabric Cream silk.

Embroidery Individual trees can be depicted using either Pekinese stitch, Pekin knot or other stitches.

Colours Combine the following colours for the trees: Olive Green 245, 246, 247, 248 for the leaves and Olive Brown 137, 138 for the trunks or Sage green 189, 191, 193 for the leaves and Drab 47, 48, 49 for the trunks. A touch of colour can be added for the flowers, using Persian Rose 164, 165, 166.

Notes The centres of the leaves can either be dark with a light edge or vice versa.

Intricately embroidered woman's waistcoat, 19th century.

Design sheet 16 Flower basket

This lavish embroidery of a basket of flowers surrounded by swirling ribbons dates from the late 19th century and comes from a woman's garment. Embroidered on a base fabric of turquoise silk satin, it uses horizontal and diagonal satin stitch, block shading and stem stitch (for the golden tassel at the bottom).

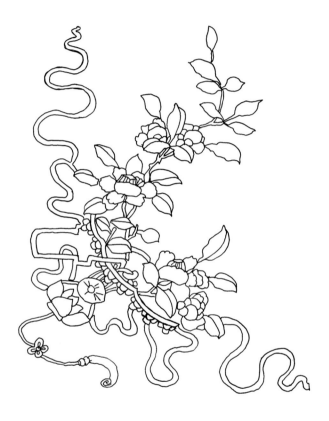

Base fabric Turquoise silk satin.
Embroidery Satin stitch variations and stem stitch.
Colours A stylized lotus flower is used to depict a basket that holds peonies among swirling ribbons. Lotus base and left pink flower in Rose 79, 80, 81; right flower and tassel in Maize Gold 95, 97, 98; cord in China blue 209; bow on cord in Dull Blue 158; leaves 157, 158, 159; blue flowers in China Blue 207, 209, 1210; edge of basket in Blue Violet 42.

Alternative colours The base colours can be replaced with spaced dyed threads as follows: Lotus base and left pink flower in Victoria Rose; right flower and tassel in Harvest Gold; blue flowers and cord in Crystal Waters; leaves and bow on cord in Aegean Sea; edge of basket in Ultra Violet.

This blue silk satin jacket, dating from the late 19th century, has its original li shui border missing. The design, depicting auspicious symbols of peonies, stylized bats and butterflies, has been embroidered in shades of blue. These designs can also be found on several other items of clothing, embroidered in multi-coloured shades.

Chapter Four
Symbols and motifs in Chinese embroidery

The individual designs found in traditional Chinese embroidery and other decorative aspects of Chinese life are laden with symbolic meanings. Plants and animals, each with their particular symbolic significance, were a very popular choice for designs and were used extensively on a variety of decorative household goods and clothing.

Dragon robes

Among many items, costumes such as dragon robes were elaborately decorated with auspicious designs and symbols in a variety of embroidery techniques. The imperial robes carried twelve symbols associated with the emperor.

The twelve Imperial Symbols

Also known as the twelve ornaments, these were displayed on the dragon robes and they not only carried judicial and cosmic significance but also conveyed the authority of the emperor. The emperor himself is identified as a symbol – the son of heaven. He stood for supreme power and was deemed to be superhuman and divine in essence. The individual symbols could either be used on their own or in a group, and they also appeared on other imperial textiles. The exceptions were the sun, the moon and the stars; these were reserved only for the emperor. When grouped together on dragon robes, the symbols were thought to express the emperor's symbolic rule over the universe.

1 Sun: East

The sun, or active principle, was associated with the power and energy fertilizing the earth and also represented heaven and intellectual enlightenment. The sun is usually depicted as a red disc containing a three-legged bird (phoenix), set over stylized clouds. This bird is representative of the yang, hence the uneven number of legs. Originally the animal associated with the sun was a type of crow, but on Qing robes, a cock was usually depicted or a phoenix, which represented the Imperial and Taoist symbols of nobility.

2 Moon: West

The moon with the hare stands for the passive principle and represents the symbol of infinite sacrifice. In the moon lives the hare, which prepares the elixir of life or drug of immortality, under the cassia tree, using a pestle and mortar (see page 106). The colour of the moon disc is described as either moon-white or light blue.

3 Stars: South (heaven)

A constellation of stars represents heaven or the heart of China (in other words, the heart of the son of heaven). It is normally depicted with three golden disks or small circles joined by 45-degree lines, to form a triangle, similar to the three-star groups of Orion, Musca and Draco. The triangle is a symbol of the eternal unity of the sun, moon and earth, a Taoist concept of the universe. This design could also be regarded as a simplified sign of the Great Bear. On the Imperial robes of the Ming Dynasty, they were shown with all seven stars of the Great Bear.

4 Mountain: North (earth)

The mountain, symbolizing the centre of the world, is represented by a rock. The Chinese consider some mountains as sacred. When they are depicted with bronze cups, water weed, fire and millet, the symbolic meaning represents the five elements of metal, water, fire, wood and earth. It also stands for steadfastness and longevity.

Opposite Li shui border taken from the bottom of a dragon robe, in which many auspicious symbols have been placed, including a bat (top), musical stone (centre, above waves), lozenges (left, in waves) and pearls (along the tops of the waves). Courtesy of Meg Andrews.

5 Dragon (lung)

Of all the mythical animals, the dragon is the most important, and is generally depicted as a serpentine monster blended of several creatures. The dragon stands as a symbol of imperial authority and embodies the personification of the great forces of nature. In spring it ascends the skies and in autumn it buries itself in the watery depths of the ocean. As nine was designated as an imperial number, the dragon was represented in nine forms. It had the head of a camel, horns of a deer, eyes of a rabbit, ears of a cow, neck of a snake, belly of a frog, scales of a carp, claws of a hawk and palms of a tiger. The scales along its back were 81 (9 × 9) in number. Those on its throat lay towards the head and those on its head were meant to look like the ridges of a mountain chain. It also had nine distinct offshoots, including whiskers at each side of the mouth and the beard under its chin.

There are several species of dragon in Chinese lore; three of the better-known species are described below.

- *Lung* is the most powerful and lives in the sky.
- *Li* is depicted with no horns and lives in the ocean.
- *Chiao* is scaly and lives in the marshes and in mountain dens.

The most frequently depicted is the celestial dragon *(ti'en lung)*. The earliest known dragons appear during the Ming Dynasty (1368–1644).

6 Pheasant (flowery bird) or a pair of pheasants

The kingdom of birds is represented by the pheasant (many-coloured bird), a symbol of literary refinement or education. Its beauty and variety of colours was said to set a good example for practising various virtues.

7 Two temple cups or bronze cups of sacrifice: West (metal)

These sacrificial cups consist of two bronze goblets or ancestral wine vessels, traditionally decorated with the

The sun

The moon

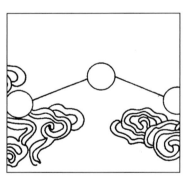

The stars

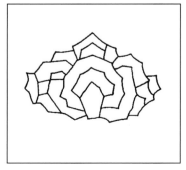

Mountain

Dragon

Pheasant

images of a tiger and a monkey. The West is influenced by metal and its season is autumn. Its colour is white, traditionally worn for mourning. The cups are also deemed to symbolize the Confucian concept of filial piety.

8 Water weed: North

The water plant is shown as a winding stem with small leaves, in a round or square motif. The North governs the element of water, symbolic of purity, and is represented by the tortoise and the colour black.

9 Millet or grain: East (wood)

This symbol is normally represented by a number of yellow seeds on a round white disk. It symbolizes the emperor's responsibility to feed the people. Together with the mountains, it represents the wood- or plant-life of the world. The East is dominated by wood, a symbol of the dragon, and marks the spring's quarter. The colour attached to the East is blue. Green was classified as a shade of blue.

10 Fire: South

This motif is depicted as a stylized dancing flame, rising in the centre and with sparks on either side, placed on a round or square motif. It is a symbol of intellectual spirit and brilliance. The element of fire is represented by the colour red, with the great bird of the south as its emblem.

11 Axe

This implement is a ritual weapon that represents the power of the emperor to pass judgment and administer punishment. It is also the emblem of a warrior.

12 Fu (geometric symbol)

This geometric design is said to derive from the prehistoric character for happiness and is the symbol of division. Generally depicted as a mirror image, this motif is arranged back to back as a double figure. It is also representative of the dualistic principles of good and evil (associated with yin and yang).

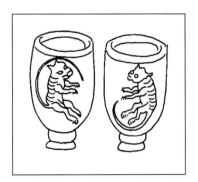

Temple cups

Water weed

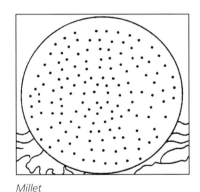

Millet

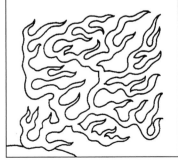

Fire

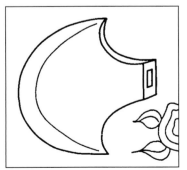

Axe

Fu *symbol*

The secular Eight Precious Things

Referred to also as the eight jewels, a term that leaves a certain amount of room for interpretation, these symbols were secular in nature. Their literary and artistic meanings reflect strong Confucian overtones. Originally, they may have been carefully described, but by the time of the Qing Dynasty, one could choose from a much wider use of jewels, which could be combined at will. The jewels represent wealth and prosperity and are generally depicted floating on the waves. This is because, according to an old belief, the sea is the source of all riches. The jewels were also used to form a set of good-luck symbols and to represent the great delight of human existence. Sometimes not all the eight motifs were used, individual ones being repeated several times instead.

Symbols 4 and 8, the painting and the artemisia leaf, were rarely depicted on robes.

1 Pearl – a jewel

This symbol, depicted either in a group or on its own, is believed to grant wishes.

2 Cash (or coin)

One or two circular ornaments, also depicted as copper coins decorated with ribbons, represent prosperity.

3 Open lozenge

This symbol, also sometimes depicted as two square-shaped golden ornaments, represents victory.

4 Painting or mirror

This symbol, sometimes depicted as a solid lozenge, represents art.

Pearl

Cash (or coin)

Open lozenge

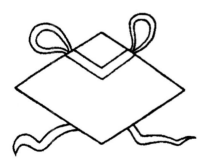

Painting or mirror

5 Musical stone

The symbol of musical accomplishment.

6 Pair of books

Sometimes depicted as two bolts of silk or scroll paintings, this symbol represents scholarly learning.

7 Pair of rhinoceros-horn cups

This should probably be interpreted as a symbol of good health, as it looks similar to rhinoceros horns, which were a costly aphrodisiac and valued for medicinal purposes.

8 Artemisia leaf

Artemisia was considered to be a good omen and was used as a symbol to prevent disease. This symbol was also depicted as a branch of red coral, which grows at the bottom of the sea and flowers once in a hundred years. Coral stood for long life and official promotion.

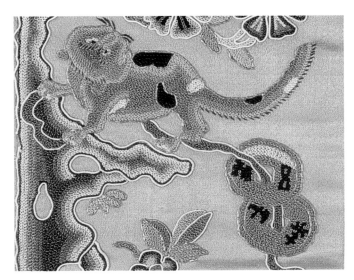

Above *Coins depicted threaded onto a monkey's tail, symbolizing wealth and prosperity.*

Musical stone

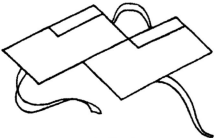

Pair of books

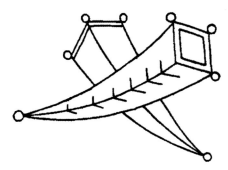

Pair of rhinoceros-horn cups

Artemisia leaf

The Buddhist Eight Precious Things

This very popular group of symbols is associated with Buddhism and known as *pa chi hsiang*. These symbols, also referred to as 'symbols of happy augury', are found extensively on Chinese embroideries, were brought from India by Buddhist missionaries and represent the spiritual attributes of the Enlightened Buddha. Four of the symbols – the canopy, the conch shell, the vase and the royal umbrella – are royal emblems associated with Buddha. The other four are symbols for religious tenets. Sometimes, the eight Buddhist symbols are mixed with the eight Taoist motifs. In addition to embroidery entwined with ribbons, the motifs were also made of wood, used in architecture and depicted on porcelain.

1 Canopy

The canopy of state, which is generally depicted as lavishly decorated with jewelled streamers and tassels, is carried over Buddha's image and holds a similar meaning to the parasol (see below). It is a symbol for a monarch and also represents purity. The canopy was seen to shelter all living beings and stands for victory over the other religions of the world.

2 Parasol (or state umbrella)

Parasols were carried over the heads of dignitaries in processions and so the symbol came to represent nobility, sovereignty or an incorruptible official.

The symbols on these two pages are taken from a richly embroidered panel, originally dating from the early part of the 19th century but extensively renovated during the 20th century. All the Buddhist symbols are present in the design, embroidered in satin stitches and outlined with single or double couched gold threads. The panel is also shown on pages 102–103. Above are shown the Canopy (left) and the Parasol (right).

3 Sacred vase

The vase holds the water of life (*amrita*), believed to be an elixir from heaven. It is also called the 'treasury of all desires'.

4 Conch shell

Used as a trumpet, this motif is often mounted with bronze or silver and represents the voice of Buddha calling the faithful to worship. One of the emblems of royalty, it is also a symbol of victory and is known as the 'blessedness of turning to right'.

5 Lotus flower

The lotus represents purity because the delicate flower rises unsullied through muddy water. It also stands as a symbol of creative power, of Buddha, who is often represented sitting in an open blossom, and of Guanyin, the goddess of mercy.

6 The sacred wheel of law

The sacred wheel of law, or karma, represents the ever-turning wheel of transmigration and the law that symbolizes the teachings of Buddha.

7 Pair of fishes

This is a symbol of domestic felicity, happiness and fertility. A pair of fishes was used as a Chinese symbol as far back as the Zhou dynasties (1027–256 BC), long before Buddhism was introduced in China.

8 Endless knot

Also referred to as the mystic knot or the lucky diagram, this is a symbol of long life. It also represents the intestines or Buddha's entrails (*zang*: infinite mercy of Buddha) and also signifies the Buddhist path, in that it represents the thread that guides one towards happiness.

Sacred vase

Conch shell

Lotus flower

Sacred wheel of law

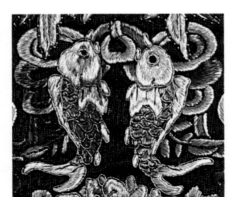

Pair of fishes

Endless knot

The Taoist Eight Precious Things

This set of precious things, also known as 'attributes of the eight Taoist immortals', symbolize eight Taoist patron saints. Taoism is a system of abstract thought which extols the virtues of inaction as a means of accomplishing everything. The Eight Immortals (*pa hsien*) – six men and two women – are legendary Taoist beings said to have lived at various times and attained immortality by studying nature's secrets. They represent the different conditions in life: poverty, wealth, aristocracy, plebeianism, age, youth, masculinity and femininity. The figures and motifs are often used as decorative elements on a wide range of items. They may be depicted as a group (each carrying his or her respective motif) or as individual figures; alternatively they may be represented simply by their motifs.

1 Fan

Zhong Li Quan, the chief of the immortals, is said to have discovered the elixir of life. He is depicted as a fat man with a bare belly, holding a peach in one hand. In the other hand he holds a fan, used to revive the dead. He is the patron saint of the military.

2 Bamboo tube and rods

Zhang Guo Lao, a recluse with supernatural powers, rides a white mule backwards. He is depicted with a type of musical instrument in the shape of a bamboo tube or a drum, with two rods to beat the drum. He is regarded as the patron saint of artists and calligraphers.

3 Sword

Lu Dong Bin is a scholar warrior worshipped by the sick. In his right hand he holds a fly-brush and a sword is slung across his back. He is said to have overcome ten temptations and to have been invested with a supernatural sword that is used to rid the world of evil. He is the patron saint of barbers.

4 Castanets

Cao Guo Jiu is depicted wearing an official robe and a court dress. He carries a pair of castanets in his hands. The brass oblong slabs, also called 'sounding plates', are said to be the court tablets that give him free access to the palace owing to his high birth. He is the patron saint of actors.

5 Crutch and gourd

Li Tie Guai, the patron saint of the sick, is represented as a beggar leaning on an iron staff, holding a pilgrim's gourd from which a scroll is escaping. The gourd is a symbol of mystery and is used to ward off evil. When dried, it becomes very durable and useful as a container. Some purses and paper lanterns are made using the gourd shape.

6 Flute

Han Xiang Zi wanders the country playing his flute, which attracts birds and beasts. He has the power to make flowers blossom and grow, and is the patron saint of musicians.

7 Basket of peaches (or flowers)

Lan Cai He is a woman dressed in a blue gown with one foot bare and the other shod. She carries a flower basket and is the patron saint of florists and gardeners.

8 Lotus pod

He Xian Gu is the daughter of a shopkeeper and carries a lotus pod in her hand. She is sometimes depicted floating on a lotus petal and holding a fly-whisk. She is said to help in managing the house and is regarded as the patron saint of housewives.

Zhong Li Quan

Zhang Guo Lao

Lu Dong Bin

Cao Guo Jiu

Li Tie Guai

Han Xiang Zi

Lan Cai He

He Xian Gu

Rebus motifs and other symbols

The use of simple motifs based on words in a rebus vocabulary was fashionable during the later Qing Dynasty (1644–1911). A rebus is a puzzle in which words and sounds are represented using pictures. The Chinese language has a limited number of sounds and is therefore a rich source of rebus possibilities. As the differences in tone do not count, the possibilities of word games are therefore endless. The most common of these visual word games is the depiction of bats (see page 117).

 # Chinese plant symbols

In Chinese culture, the social context in which symbols were used was important. Plant motifs on textiles and craft items offered a means of communicating in a situation where words would have been regarded as primitive. Most of the motifs were stylized, and their symbolic meanings were either derived from the characteristics or properties of the plant.

Bamboo

The bamboo is known as 'the friend of China'. Due to its durability and the sturdy nature that enables it to survive winter, it is thought to bend before life's troubles and stands for long friendship. The bamboo also represents long life because it is evergreen and as the plant is hollow, with drooping leaves, it is said to represent the virtue of modesty. When bamboo is depicted with the peach and the pine, it conveys the ideology of long life.

Chrysanthemum (China aster)

This flower has many symbolic interpretations, including friendship, joviality, long life and endurance. It is also associated with a life of ease because the poet Tao Ch'ien (365–427), instead of taking an official post, chose a life of poverty devoted to writing and growing chrysanthemums. It represents autumn, being the plant chosen for the ninth month of the old Chinese calendar, known as chrysanthemum month, and it is a traditional custom to pick this flower on the ninth day of that month. Different

Chrysanthemum

Peony

Finger lemon

types of chrysanthemum are given fine and exquisite names. For example, the yellow button is called 'heaven full of stars'; the white quill is called 'goose feathers tube'; the yellow quill is called 'carrot threads'; the large ragged mauve is called 'drunk with wine made from peaches of the immortal'. The big single white flower with a yellow centre is called 'jade saucer gold cup' and the ones with fine petals are called 'pine needles' or 'dragon's beard'.

Finger lemon

This inedible yet fragrant-smelling citrus fruit is frequently used to scent rooms. The fruits look like fingers, and as their shape has been likened to the classic form of Buddha's hands, it is also known as 'Buddha's hand'. The finger lemon represents long life and also wealth, as the shape is said to look as if it is holding money.

Mushroom

This fungus was ground and mixed into the Taoist elixir of long life. The shape recurs in the head of the auspicious five-hued cloud motif.

Narcissus

This flower is called the 'water fairy'. As it blooms around the New Year, it is used as a lucky symbol for the coming year and it also represents a married couple. When a narcissus is depicted with bamboo and stones, the play on words could mean 'The immortals wish you long life'.

Orchid

Much worn by the Empress Dowager, who was called 'the Orchid', this flower is an appropriate emblem of beauty, love and refinement.

Peach

Food of life and the nourishment of the eight immortal Taoist saints, the peach is a symbol of long life. This symbolic meaning is based on the legend of the peach tree of immortality, said to have grown in the garden of the fairy goddess Xi-Wang-Mu, the Holy Queen of the West, in the far Kulun Mountains. The tree was said to blossom once every 3,000 years, yielding a peach of immortality, which took another 3,000 years to ripen. The peach also represents marriage: in China, the tree blossoms in springtime, an auspicious time for getting married.

Peony

The peony is regarded as the queen of all flowers and stands for wealth and distinction. When the peony is represented in conjunction with flowers from the fragrant olive (*Olea fragrans*), it is emblematic of high rank.

Pine tree

This is a symbol of long life and steadfastness and has similar meanings to the bamboo.

Plum

The ordinary plum symbolizes good fortune, while the wild plum represents the harshness of winter.

Plum blossom

As the plum blooms in snow, its blossom stands for perseverance.

Pomegranate

This is a symbol of fertility and plenty of children, as the numerous pink pips are said to guarantee many sons.

Willow

This tree has many female connotations. For example, a beautiful woman's waist could be likened to a willow, or her eyebrows to the curve of willow leaves. A young girl could be referred to as a young willow, and an old woman as a faded willow.

Plants representing the 12 months of the year

January	Plum blossom
February	Peach
March	Peony
April	Cherry
May	Magnolia
June	Pomegranate
July	Lotus
August	Pear
September	Mallow
October	Chrysanthemum
November	Gardenia
December	Poppy

Flowers of the four seasons

Spring	tree peony and magnolia
Summer	lotus
Autumn	chrysanthemum
Winter	plum blossom and rose

Combined plant symbols

Using rebus motifs, plants are often represented in conjunction with other plants or symbols. Examples of some of these combinations include:

- Pine, bamboo and peach convey long life.

- Pine, bamboo and plum are known as the 'three friends of winter' because they stay green in cold weather and are generally found grouped together.

- Plum, orchid, bamboo and chrysanthemum are known as the 'four gentlemen'.

- Peach, pomegranate and the finger lemon are known as the 'three plenties', the 'three fruits' or the 'three abundances'. They stand for children, years and happiness.

Left *20th-century panel of a lotus flower in a vase. The lotus flower symbolizes purity.*

Animal and bird symbols

Animals have played a part in Chinese astronomy for centuries, and both mythical and actual animals figure as symbols. The most popular and prolific animal designs are those featuring bats.

Bats

The Chinese words for bat and for happiness are the same (*fu*). Sometimes the designs for bats are so ornate that they look like butterflies (see page 60). So popular is the bat theme, that different bat motifs carry distinct meanings. For example, the depiction of two bats represents long life, four bats together means four joys, while five bats stand for five blessings (long life, wealth and riches, love of virtue, peacefulness and a happy death). The five bats also stand for five happinesses or the blessings of old age. A bat depicted with peaches (which are known as a symbol of long life) means 'May you live long and be happy'.

The rebus for red bats takes the theme a bit further as red (*hong*) is a lucky colour. The word *hong* can also mean majestic or sublime.

Sometimes bats are depicted carrying symbols in their mouths. For example a bat carrying a musical stone (*fu qing*) means happiness and prosperity. A bat with a swastika (*wan fu*) means 'ten thousand times happiness'.

Butterfly

Another very popular motif is the butterfly (*tieh*), which is also identical to the term that denotes 70–80 years old. Because of this, depicting a butterfly shows the desire to reach a great age. The butterfly is also a symbol of a happy marriage and may be regarded as the Chinese Cupid.

When two butterflies are depicted flying towards each other, this signifies a meeting between two people.

Right *The butterfly, symbol of the desire to live to a great old age.*

Qi lin

This mythical creature is a strange-looking monster blended of ox, dragon and deer, with horns and flames springing from its body. Its appearance is rare and it heralds either the coming of a wise ruler or the birth of a sage. It is the symbol used to represent the first rank of military officials.

Cock

This bird embodies *yang* and stands for warmth and the life of the universe. It is associated with the following virtues:

- The crown on its head is a symbol of literary spirit.
- The spurs on its feet symbolize its warlike disposition.
- It has courage because it fights its enemies.
- Its benevolence is witnessed by its perpetual clucking.
- It is faithful, as it keeps the hours.

A red cock protects against fire, while a white cock is placed on coffins to clear the roads of demons. When a cock is depicted with a hen in a garden among rocks and peonies, the pair is regarded as a symbol representing the pleasures of country life.

Deer

This animal is said to live to a very great age and is allegedly the only animal able to find the sacred fungus of immortality. A deer is meant to represent official emolument (wages).

Elephant

Sacred to Buddhism, the elephant is a symbol of strength, prudence and power and is the bearer of the wish-granting gem. It is often portrayed carrying lucky objects, such as branches of coral and musical stones. The elephant also carries on its back the alm bowl of Buddha.

Lion

The lion, as represented in Chinese art, is a mixture of a lion and a spaniel. It is generally shown supporting a ball of some woven material. Large stone figures of lions are placed as guardians at the gates of Buddhist temples. For this reason, the lion is referred to familiarly as the 'dog of Fo' (*Fo* means 'Buddha').

Ram

This symbol denotes a successful official career. When three rams are depicted, this announces the coming of spring or the start of the New Year.

Tiger

The tiger, lord of waters and king of beasts, is the enemy of the dragon and is often depicted in conflict with it.

Crane

The crane, regarded as the head of the feathered tribe, represents long life. The white Manchurian crane is said to have a life span of 2000 years, after which time it is supposed to turn entirely black. It is used on mandarin

Above *Ram, taken from an embroidered panel (possibly 18th century or earlier). Courtesy of Meg Andrews.*

badges for officials of the first rank. The crane, the deer and the tortoise are sometimes depicted together, as a combined symbol of long life.

Pair of Mandarin ducks

Mandarin ducks are so called because of their magnificent plumage and their superiority over other ducks. When paired, they become attached to each other as life companions and when separated, they pine away and die. As such, they are regarded as symbolic of conjugal bliss.

Peacock

This represents beauty and dignity. The Manchus used peacock feathers in a variety of ways to denote rank.

Phoenix

The phoenix (*feng huang*) is depicted as a beautifully coloured bird compounded of several species. This mythical creature is said to have five human qualities: its head represents virtue, its wings duty, its back denotes correct behaviour, its breast symbolizes humanity and its stomach reliability. It is a symbol associated with the empress and a phoenix is often depicted on wedding dresses, holding the meaning that the wearer is an Empress for a day. If a picture has a dragon on the left and a phoenix on the right, this is a symbol of man and wife. In Chinese mythology, the appearance of a phoenix is said to be auspicious and to herald the coming of a virtuous and just ruler.

Above *Manchurian Cranes, 20th century, from a fine embroidery in the Su style from Suzhou. These elegant birds are said to represent long life.*
Courtesy of Alan McIntyre.

Other symbols

Fish

The Chinese word for fish *(yu)* is the same as that for 'abundance'. This is a symbol of literary eminence or success in exams. On an engagement, one of the articles presented to the future bride's family is a brace of fish. Various species of fish are used as symbols. The carp, for example, is admired for its struggle against the current and means perseverance. The sturgeon is said to be successful in passing the rapids when it swims up the Yellow River each year, and can transform itself into a dragon. When goldfishes, a goldfish bowl and peonies are put together, it is symbolic of wealth.

Flaming pearl

The flaming pearl, symbolizing good luck and granting of wishes, is called *lung-chu* in Chinese, 'the pearl of the dragon', and its centre sometimes contains the prehistoric character for thunder. When combined with stylized flames it conveyed the idea of thunder and lightning, thus intensifying the symbolic meaning of the awesome power of the dragon, ruler of heaven.

Ruyi sceptre

Ruyi stands for 'as you wish'. It is a kind of short sword made of iron and when given as a gift it meant good wishes for prosperity to the recipient. The shape of the head of the *ruyi* may be derived from the sacred fungus, referred to as the plant of longevity. This design is often depicted as a border pattern or individual motif, not only on textiles but also on porcelain, buildings and other objects. The motif is also comparable to a stylized bat.

Above *The flaming pearl, signifying good luck, is often depicted with dragons. This detail is taken from the image on page 95.*

Above *The head of a Ruyi sceptre, shown among pearls and waves in a Li Shui border. Taken from the image on page 105.*

Above *Shou symbol, meaning good luck, used as a border in a Mandarin badge of rank. The whole image is shown on page 37.*

Above *Bat carrying a swastika in its mouth, taken from the same embroidered panel that is shown on pages 102–103.*

Shou

This is a common character, meaning long life, and is represented in countless forms of stylization. Often the swastika motif is concealed within the stylization of this character, so that the meaning of long life is doubled.

Stylized flames

This design, used on dragon robes and mandarin squares and in Buddhist art, was meant to indicate the mystical or mythical nature of fire, lightning or consuming energy.

Swastika

One of the oldest known designs, this became a Buddhist symbol of good luck in about 2000 BC. It is the shortened form for 10,000 and its meanings include long life.

Thunder line

Originating in the Shang Dynasty or perhaps even earlier, this comes from the prehistoric Chinese character for thunder. It is used as a border motif or as a background and looks like the continuous running series of rounded spiral or square shapes. It can also be formed into S-curved shapes, as in the scroll type. Thunder was important as it brought rain, a heaven-sent gift of abundance that was essential for agriculture.

Vase

One of the basic shapes of the vase was apparently fashioned from the form of the feminine curve. The word for vase (*ping*) is the same as the word peace. When a rare vase was given as a gift, it was meant to symbolize peace-keeping.

Yin and yang

A cosmic symbol depicted in a circle, the shaded side (*yin*) represents the female principle, while the pale side (*yang*) represents the male, light and heaven. The yin and yang are bisected in the middle by a curving S-shaped line. The whole symbol signifies the balance of opposites inherent in all of nature – male and female, light and dark, good and evil, sun and moon, cold and heat and so on. Yin is the procreative element of nature and Yang is the creative element.

Clouds

A symbol of good luck and happiness, this is deemed to be more auspicious if represented by more than one colour. When depicted as a five-hued cloud motif it stands for great peace. Usually the five colours associated with this symbol are red, violet, blue, green and yellow.

The four treasures

Referred to as the four precious articles or invaluable gems, these consist of ink, paper, brush-pen and ink slab.

The ten longevities

The ten symbols of longevity are the bamboo, clouds, deer, Manchurian crane, mountains, pine, sacred fungus, sun, tortoise and water waves.

Above *Uncut sleeveband, dating from around 1800, in fine silk threads on a faded pale green fabric. This exquisite embroidery would have been used to decorate the edge of a robe belonging to a woman of high birth. The scene is composed of four pairs of birds amid flowering plum blossoms, peonies and lotus flowers.*

Chronology

Neolithic period	*c.* **7000–***c.* **1600** BC
(Xia Dynasty)	*c.* 2100–*c.* 1600 BC
Shang Dynasty	*c.* **1600–1027** BC
Western Zhou	**1027–771** BC
Eastern Zhou	**770–256** BC
Spring and Autumn Annals period	770–476 BC
Warring States period	475–221 BC
Qin Dynasty	**221–206** BC
Western Han	**206** BC**–8** AD
Xin Dynasty (Wang Mang interregnum)	**9–23** AD
Eastern Han	**25–220**
Three Kingdoms period	**220–280**
Western Jin	**265–316**
Eastern Jin	**317–420**
Northern and Southern Dynasties	**420–580**
Northern Dynasties	
Northern Wei	386–534
Eastern Wei	534–550
Western Wei	535–556
Northern Qi	550–577
Northern Zhou	557–580
Southern Dynasties	
Song	420–479
Qi	479–502
Liang	502–557
Chen	557–589
Sui Dynasty	**581–618**
Tang Dynasty	**618–907**
Five Dynasties period	**907–960**
Liao Dynasty	**907–1125**
Song Dynasty	**960–1279**
Northern Song	960–1127
Southern Song	1127–1279
Jin Dynasty	**1115–1234**
Yuan Dynasty	**1279–1368**
Ming Dynasty	**1368–1644**
Qing Dynasty	**1644–1911**
Republic of China	**1911–1949**
People's Republic of China	**1949–present**

Useful addresses
UK

Pearsall's
Silk threads
Tancred Street
Taunton
Somerset
TA1 1RY
Tel: 01823 274 700
www.pearsallsembroidery.co.uk
Email: sales@pearsallsembroidery.com

Embroidery East West
Chinese silk floss, fabrics, threads, frames and kits
Mail order only
Tel/fax: 020 8851 4695
www.embroideryeastwest.co.uk
Email: embroideryeastwest@hotmail.com

Mulberry Silks
Silk threads
2 The Old Rectory Cottages
Easton Grey
Malmesbury
Wiltshire
SN16 0PE
Tel: 01666 840 881
www.mulberrysilks-patriciawood.com

Rainbow Silks
Silk fabrics and threads, dyes etc.
6 Wheelers Yard
High Street
Great Missenden
Buckinghamshire
HP16 0AL
www.rainbowsilks.co.uk
Email: Caroline@rainbowsilks.co.uk

Golden Threads
Specialist range of gold threads
Spotted Cow Cottage
Broad Oak
Heathfield
East Sussex
TN21 8UE
Tel: 01435 862 810
www.goldenthreads.co.uk
Email: goldenthreadsuk@lineone.net

Barnyarns
Stands, frames, magnets and other needlework materials
Brickyard Road
Boroughbridge
North Yorkshire
YO51 9NS
Tel: 01423 326 423
Email: sales@barnyarns.com

Restore Products
Conservation materials (glue, needles, acid-free paper etc.)
2 Talbot Road
Bowden
Altricham
Cheshire
WA14 3JD
Tel/fax: 0161 928 0020
Email: products@textilerestoration.co.uk

Hanshan Tang Books Ltd
Specialist and rare books
Unit 3 Ashburton Centre
276 Cortis Road
London
SW15 3AY
Tel: 020 8788 4464
www.hanshan.com
Email: hst@hanshan.com

The Old Bookshop
Specialist embroidery books
36 Gordon Road
Enfield
Middlesex
EN2 7PD
Tel: 020 8637 1661
Email: felicity@fgwarnes.u-net.com

Meg Andrews
Antique textiles
www.meg-andrews.com
Email: megandrews@clara.co.uk

Whaleys (Bradford) Ltd
Fabrics
Harris Court Mills
Great Horton
Bradford
West Yorkshire
BD7 4EQ
Tel: 01274 576 718
www.whaleys-bradford.ltd.uk

USA

Tristan Brook Designs
Pearsall's Filoselle thread suppliers
Barbara Jackson
182 Green Glade
Memphis, TN 38120
Email: tris@midsouth.rr.com

Access Commodities Inc.
Threads and fabrics
PO Box 1355
1299 South Virginia Street
Terrell, TX 75160
Tel: (001) 792 563 3313

Treadleart
Threads and fabrics
95834 Narbonne Avenue
Lomita, CA 90717
www.ylicorp.com
Email: ylicorp@ylicorp.com

SCS USA
Threads and fabrics
9631 Colefax Street
Portland, OR 97220-1232
Tel: (001) 503 252 1452

Australia

The Thread Studio
Threads and fabrics
6 Smith Street
Perth
WA 6000
Australia
www.thethreadstudio.com
Email: mail@thethreadstudio.com

New Zealand

Margaret Barnet Distributors Ltd
Threads and fabrics
19 Beasley Avenue
PO Box 12-034
Penrose
Auckland
New Zealand

Opposite page *Part of a sleeveband depicting children playing, early 19th century.*

Bibliography

Embroidery

Baker, M. and M. Lunt. *Blue and white: the cotton embroideries of rural China.* Sidgwick and Jackson, London, 1978.

Ho Wing Meng. *Straits Chinese beadwork and embroidery: a collector's guide.* Times Books International, Singapore, 1994.

Hu Weimin, ed. Xu Huping. *Embroidery (Zhixiu): Gems of collections in Nanjing Museum.* Shanghai Chinese Classics Publishing House, Shanghai, 1999.

de Saint-Aubin, C. G. *Art of the embroiderer: designer to the king.* Los Angeles County Museum of Art, Los Angeles, 1983. Translation of Charles Germain de Saint-Aubin, *L'art du brodeur: dessignateur de roi,* 1770.

Dowdey, Patrick. *Threads of light: Chinese embroidery from Suzhou and the photography of Robert Glenn Ketchum.* Fowler Museum of Cultural History, Los Angeles, 1999.

Lemon, Jane. *Metal thread embroidery.* B T Batsford, London, 1987.

Mailey, Jean. *Embroidery of Imperial China.* China Institute in America, New York, 1978.

Thomas, Mary. *Dictionary of embroidery stitches.* Hodder and Stoughton, London, 1936.

Wang Yarong. *Chinese folk embroidery.* Thames and Hudson, London, 1987.

Westphal, Katherine. *Dragons and other creatures: Chinese embroidery of the Ch'ing dynasty.* Lancaster-Miller Publishers, California, 1979.

Young C. Chung. *The art of oriental embroidery: history, aesthetics and techniques.* Bell and Hyman, London, 1980.

Wang, Loretta. *The Chinese purse: embroidered purses of the Ch'ing dynasty.* Taiwan, 1986.

Asian embroideries: Asian Art Museum of San Francisco.

Cixiu (Embroidery) National Palace Museum

Shanghai People's Fine Arts. Embroidery – a collection of best artistic works.

Symbols and motifs

Eberhard, Wolfram. *A dictionary of Chinese symbols.* Routledge and Kegan Paul, London, 1986.

Vuilleumier, Bernard. *Symbolism of Chinese imperial ritual robes: the art of silk weaving in China.* The China Institute, London, 1939.

Williams, C. A. S. *Outlines of Chinese Symbolism and Art Motives.* Kelly and Walsh Ltd., Shanghai, 1932.

Chinese costumes and textiles

Cammann, Schuyler. 'Development of the Mandarin square', *Harvard Journal of Asiatic Studies,* Vol. 8 No. 2, Harvard Yenching Institure, Cambridge, Massachusetts, 1944.

Cammann, Schuyler. *China's dragon robes.* The Ronald Press, New York, 1952.

Christie, Anthony. *Chinese mythology.* Chancellor Press, London, 1968.

Claris F. and H. Brown. *Silken robes from China.* Cheltenham Art Gallery and Museum, Cheltenham, 1987.

Coleman, Teresa. *Dragons and silk from the Forbidden City: the genius of China.* Odyssey Publications Ltd, Union Lake, Michigan, 1998.

Corrigan, Gina. *Miao textiles from China.* British Museum Press, London, 2001.

Dickinson, G. and L. Wrigglesworth. *Imperial wardrobe.* Bamboo Publishing, 1990.

Eracle, Jean. *Costume Chinois de l'epoque T'sing (Chinese costume from the Qing era).* Musée d'ethonographie, Geneva, 1978.

Eberhard, Wolfram. *A history of China.* Routledge and Kegan Paul, London, 1997.

Gao Hanyu, tr. Rosemary Scott and Susan Whitfield. *Chinese textile designs.* Penguin, London, 1992.

Garrett, Valery M. *A collector's guide to Chinese dress accessories.* Times Editions, Singapore, 1997.

Garrett, Valery M. *Chinese clothing: an illustrated guide.* Oxford University Press, New York, 1994.

Huang, N. and J. Chen. *Zhongguo lidai zhuanghshi wenyang (Design of Chinese adornment).* Beijing, 1999.

Hucker, Charles. *China's imperial past.* Duckworth, London, 1980.

Huxley, Francis. *The dragon: nature of spirit, spirit of nature.* Thames and Hudson, London, 1979.

Jackson, Beverley. *Splendid slippers: a thousand years of an erotic tradition.* Ten Speed Press, Berkeley, 1997.

Jackson, Beverley. *Kingfisher blue: treasures of an ancient Chinese art.* Ten Speed Press, Berkeley, 2001.

Jacobsen, Robert D. *Imperial silks: Ching Dynasty textiles in the Minneapolis Institute of Arts.* Volumes 1 and 2. Minneapolis Institute of Arts, 2002.

Minick, S. and Jiao Ping. *Arts and crafts of China.* Thames and Hudson, London, 1996.

Priest, Alan. *Costumes from the Forbidden City.* Metropolitan Museum of Art, New York, 1945.

Priest, Alan. *Imperial robes and textiles of the Chinese court.* Minneapolis Institute of Arts exhibition catalogue, April–June 1943.

Thorp, Robert L. *Son of heaven: Imperial arts of China.* Son of Heaven Press, Seattle, 1998.

Vollmer, John E. *In the presence of the dragon throne: Ch'ing dynasty costume (1644–1911) in the Royal Ontario Museum.* Royal Ontario Museum exhibition catalogue, Toronto, 1997.

Vollmer, John E. *Five colours of the universe: clothes and fabrics of the Ch'ing dynasty.* Edmonton Art Gallery exhibition catalogue, 1980.

Vollmer, John E. *Decoding dragons: status garments in Ching dynasty China.* Museum of Art, University of Oregon, 1983.

Whitfield, R. and Wang Tao. *Exploring China's past: new discoveries and studies in archaeology and art.* Saffron Books, London, 1999.

Wilson, Verity. *Chinese dress.* Bamboo Publishing, 1986.

Wood, Frances. *Chinese illustrations.* The British Library, London, 1985.

Wrigglesworth, Linda. *Making the grade: the badge of rank in China.* London 1996.

Zhou Xun and Gao Chunming. *5000 years of Chinese costumes.* The Commercial Press, Shanghai, 1987.

Art and design

ed. Applebaum, Stanley. *Traditional Chinese designs.* Dover Publications, Inc., New York, 1987.

Christopher, Barbara. *Traditional Chinese designs iron-on transfer patterns.* Dover Publications, Inc., New York, 1987.

Jablonski, Ramona. *The Chinese cut-out designs book: designs from the world of nature.* Stemmer House, Owings-Mills, Maryland, 1983.

Jourdain, M and Soames Jenyns. *Chinese export art in the eighteenth century.* Spring Books, 1967.

Levitchi, Leon. *Classical Chinese paintings.* Meridiane Publishing House, Bucharest, 1979.

Markrich, Lilo. *Oriental iron-on transfer patterns: 24 authentic embroidery motifs from the textile museum.* Dover Publications, Inc., New York, 1980.

Ming-Ju Sun. *Oriental flower designs and motifs for artists, needleworkers and craftspeople.* Dover Publications, Inc., New York, 1985.

Ed. Northeast Drama Institute, People's Republic of China. *Traditional Chinese textile designs.* Dover Publications, Inc., New York, 1980.

Chinese traditional line figural paintings. Shanghai Calligraphy and Painting Publishing House

Above *Pink peony from a dragon robe dating from around the early 19th century, embroidered in Pekin knot seed stitch.*

Index